True North Business

TRUE NORTH BUSINESS

A Leader's Guide to Extraordinary
Growth & Impact

BOBBY ALBERT

NEW YORK

LONDON • NASHVILLE • MELBOURNE • VANCOUVER

TRUE NORTH BUSINESS

A Leader's Guide to Extraordinary Growth and Impact

© 2019 Bobby Albert

Published in New York, New York, by Morgan James Publishing. Morgan James is a trademark of Morgan James, LLC. www.MorganJamesPublishing.com

ISBN 9781642791549 paperback
ISBN 9781642791556 eBook
Library of Congress Control Number: 2018907445

Cover Design by:
Marchon L. Pulido

Interior Design by:
Chris Treccani
www.3dogcreative.net

To my wife, Susan, whose support and friendship I have enjoyed for forty-five years and counting, and to our three sons, Rob, Brian, and Kyle, who are my life's legacy and of whom I'm very proud.

CONTENTS

INTRODUCTION

Are You Leading or Wandering?

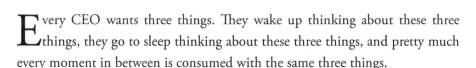

Every CEO wants three things. They wake up thinking about these three things, they go to sleep thinking about these three things, and pretty much every moment in between is consumed with the same three things.

What are those three things?

1. Results
2. Results
3. Results!

They not only want results, but they want bigger results, and they want them faster.

What kind of results do they want?

Primarily, an increase in profits.

Secondarily,

- An increase in revenue
- A decrease in expenses
- An increase in productivity

And finally,

- An increase in employee retention
- A reduction in employee absences
- An increase in customer satisfaction
- A decrease in safety violations
- A decrease in product and/or service defects

You may ask, "How do you know?"

Because, for years, I was a CEO!

Today, I mentor leaders in all kinds of organizations, and I've found that they also want the same three things.

They also tell me they would have no problem achieving the results they want—if it weren't for their employees or the tax laws or the Internet or their family . . . and the list goes on.

Bumper-Car Business

When I was a young boy, my parents would take a friend and me to spend Saturday afternoons at Funland Amusement Park near my home. It was the place to be, and we would see a bunch of our other friends there as well. I would always get a Coke and cotton candy. Yum! I can still taste that cotton candy.

My favorite ride was the bumper cars. We would have fun ramming each other (and getting rammed from behind), and when the ride was over, we'd jump out of our cars and get right back in line for another turn.

As much as I loved that experience as a kid, I admit it doesn't sound like much fun today. Yet, many leaders find themselves in exactly the same situation, resulting in what I call Bumper-Car Business.

In this always-on, always-connected world we now live in, leaders feel they're constantly being hit with crisis after crisis from every direction. Instead of leading with vision and attaining the results they want, they find themselves in survival mode, thinking reactively and focusing on what will ease their pain the fastest, just trying to avoid the next collision.

Take a True North Bearing

As a leader, do you feel like you're stuck in the bumper-car ride, hit with crisis after crisis? Do you find yourself in survival mode, doing whatever it takes to avoid the next collision?

Although it may feel like you're going nowhere, this kind of Bumper-Car Business approach will eventually take you exactly where you *don't* want to go.

Bumper-Car Business leaders are always trying to catch their competitors, concerned more about the balance in the checking account than how to better meet their customers' needs and focused on the urgent HR problem of the day instead of building a team that is aligned with their values. Then, they wonder why turnover is so high and the morale is so low.

The Bumper-Car Business approach eventually leads to losing your best employees, leaving you with only mediocre employees. This leads to lower productivity and even higher employee turnover, which increases your cost of doing business and causes a loss of customers, therefore causing revenue to drop.

The saddest part of Bumper-Car Businesses is the lost opportunity to produce incredible, unbelievable, extraordinary profits—the results most leaders were driving for in the first place.

The good news is that you can get off the bumper-car ride! You just need to find your True North.

True North Business

What do I mean by True North? If you enjoy hiking, sailing, or any other kind of orienteering, you probably know exactly what I mean. From what I understand from geologists, true north is the unchanging northern geographic point at the end of the Earth's axis. It's different from magnetic north, which shifts over time. No matter where we've been or where we're going, true north never changes.

So, when I say "True North" in the context of business leadership, I'm talking about basing your leadership on things that don't change or that at least stay relatively constant over time.

True North Business is vastly different from Bumper-Car Business. True North Business leaders know who they are, why they exist, where they're going, how to get there, and what they want to accomplish along the way.

I saw the benefits of True North Business firsthand as CEO of our family moving business, Albert Companies, from 1973 to 2011. At our company, we definitely were not perfect, but over time, we got more intentional about creating something great and enduring. Between 2005, when we clarified our True North and embraced it as a team, and 2011, when I sold the company, we saw the following results during some of the toughest economic times:

- Revenue grew about five times.
- Profit increased slightly more than five times.
- We were chosen as one of the 100 Best Companies to Work for in Texas in 2011 and 2012, the first two times we applied.

Our company experienced significant growth during the Great Recession, a time when many other companies were declining. When we got crystal clear about who we were, why we existed, where we were going, how we were going to get there, and what we wanted to accomplish along the way, extraordinary results followed.

Many leaders have come to accept merely "good" results in their business. However, if they employ the principles of True North Business, they will see *great* (as in extraordinary, unforeseen, and unbelievable) results.

Good is the enemy of great.
—JIM COLLINS

Selling my company in 2011 marked the end of my role as CEO of the Albert Companies, but it was also the beginning of my second half of life. I've since created a new business, Values-Driven Leadership, LLC, whose purpose is to "Make a Difference."

For me, this is a wonderful opportunity to go from success to significance by adding value to people not only once . . . but twice.

First, I get the opportunity to make a difference—in people, for people, and with people—by writing articles, speaking, conducting workshops, offering books and video training, mentoring executives, and consulting with business owners and leaders.

Second, my wife and I have also been blessed to create The Bobby and Susan Albert Foundation, a 501(c)(3) organization, so that any future profits from this new business will go into the foundation, allowing us to financially support organizations and causes of similar core values.

Finding my True North not only produced the business performance we wanted but also created a meaningful legacy. And it can do the same for you.

The One Person You Can Change

The world as we have created it is a process of our thinking. It cannot be changed without changing our thinking.
—ALBERT EINSTEIN

One of the reasons people get stuck in Bumper-Car Business and don't achieve their dreams is that they desire to change their results without changing their thinking.

I have good news for you: you can get off the bumper-car ride and chart your own course as a leader. All you need is the desire, will, and self-discipline to change how you think. Consider the following truths:

- You are responsible for your own choices, and you have the freedom to choose how you respond to what you experience in life.

- You can change (if you are willing and have the desire) how you think about making choices, which will lead to more right decisions.
- You can change where you spend your time and energy—focusing more on what you can control and less on what you cannot control.

It's time to stop Googling for quick fixes to today's leadership challenges. That results in a Bumper-Car Business—bouncing off today's problems and bracing for tomorrow's. It's time to take back our personal responsibility as leaders and choose to lead ourselves *and* our businesses.

That's exactly what *True North Business* will help you do. It will teach you five proven essentials to discover True North for yourself and your business, plus reveal the path that will get you there, giving you the business results you want and establishing a meaningful legacy in the process. But, before we get into those fundamentals, there are two important things you need to know.

First, as I mentioned above, there's no quick fix to leadership problems. It takes time to change your thinking, invest in the process, and see the results. You can't master these essentials in one day or even one week. To see results, you must be committed to growth over time. That's the nature of True North Business versus Bumper-Car Business.

In this book, you'll learn how to change the only person you can actually control—yourself. If you've been frustrated by your team or your circumstances, that should sound like good news. The bad news is that you'll need to entertain the possibility that your business problems may lie with you, as the leader.

But, I have even better news. When you focus on changing your thinking as a leader and start investing in your team, leadership becomes a lot more fun. In fact, research shows that having the *right* kind of fun as a team increases innovation and insight,[1] and you'll learn more about how to do that for your own team in chapter 13.

---

1   Ian Altman, "How Playing Games Can Lead to Serious Results in Business," Forbes.com, October 3, 2017, https://www.forbes.com/sites/ianaltman/2017/10/03/how-playing-games-can-lead-to-serious-results-in-business/#30f0ce147ba3.

Second, if you want your profits to increase and your business to grow, the answer isn't pushing harder to get results at any cost. You can't get great results without investing in *relationships*.

Rather than focusing on the results, focus on investing in the people who will get you those results.

What all that means is that the leadership approach you'll learn in this book is essentially a paradox: you need to focus on yourself to change what you get from others, and you need to focus on relationships to get results. It's counter to what's being taught in most MBA programs, where they tend to focus on increasing shareholder value at all costs (and being very serious while doing it). But, I've learned in my decades of being in business and mentoring leaders that there's a better way.

In part 1, you'll learn the five essentials of True North Business:

1. Core values
2. Purpose
3. Vision
4. Super-objectives
5. Effective leadership

And, yes, we had fun with them! To share these essentials with our people, we held company-wide workshops to teach specific leadership practices and how to apply them. We even created buttons to wear to make the concepts easy to remember.

So, in parts 2, 3, and 4, you'll learn three practices to begin applying the True North Business Essentials in your own organization. We call them ON/IN, WOW!, and 1-2-3:

- ON/IN: In part 2, you'll learn the foundational strategy of working ON and IN your business regularly. You'll also receive your True North

Business roadmap to keep you on track as a leader and continually grow yourself, your team, and your business, no matter what obstacles come your way.

- WOW!: In part 3, you'll discover your purpose and vision—*why* you exist and *where* you are going, both as a leader and as an organization—and how to share them with your people in an engaging way.
- 1-2-3: In part 4, you'll learn how to use participatory leadership to invest in the people who will get you the results you want. It's your path towards True North, and it's as easy as 1-2-3.

In my previous book, *Principled Profits*, I shared key business principles that will put your organization on the road to lasting success and significance. *True North Business* further clarifies these key principles and gives you a clear strategy to put them to work in your organization.

What I'm asking you to do isn't difficult, even though it might sound unconventional or even unorthodox. You might even find yourself enjoying work again!

Are you ready to embark on this journey of True North Business? Let's get started!

PART ONE

The True North Business Essentials

Core Values
Who Are We?

Purpose
Why Do We Exist?

Effective Leadership

Vision
Where Are We Going?

Super-Objectives
What Do We Want to Accomplish Every Day?

CHAPTER 1

Core Values, Purpose, Vision, and Super-Objectives

Establish Your True North Foundation

Success is neither magical nor mysterious. Success is the natural consequence of consistently applying the basic fundamentals.
—JIM ROHN

There's a lot of emphasis today on the importance of company culture. It makes sense: if your people are happier, they'll be more productive and create better results. Many companies focus on creating culture as a goal: they provide nice amenities for their employees solely for what they'll get in return.

At our company, we approached culture differently. Our mindset was, "What can we give our people without expecting anything in return?" We wanted to do the right thing for the right reasons, no matter what.

I believe what made our company so successful was not our product or service offerings, but what our company stood for—and how our people lived it out.

Success is not in your products or services, but in what your company stands for and how your people live it out.

3

I saw the positive results of this approach grow over time, much like a fruit tree grows. A farmer plants, tends, prunes, cultivates, and grows the tree, not the fruit; the fruit is the result of the farmer's labors. If culture is the fruit, then core values, purpose, vision, and super-objectives are the roots, and effective leadership is the trunk. Cultivate the soil and feed the roots, then your organization, the "tree", will produce delicious fruit!

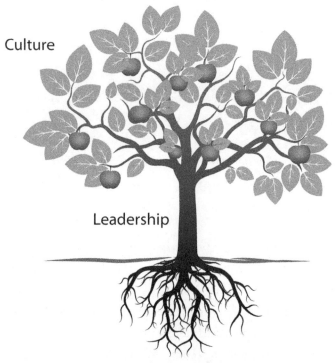

Culture

Leadership

Core Values, Purpose, Vision
& Super-Objectives

According to Stephen Covey, "People can't live with change without a changeless core."

Our organization experienced constant change—that's just my nature. The reason our people could manage this constant change long term is because they understood the changeless core.

At every company-wide meeting, I would always remind our people of the five True North Business Essentials:

1. Our core values (*who* we are)
2. Our purpose (*why* we exist)
3. Our vision (*where* we are going)
4. Our super-objectives (*what* we want to accomplish every day)
5. The principles of effective leadership (*how* we enhance relationships as we drive for results)

If you're feeling overcome by constant change, I invite you to find your changeless core.

As we adopted the True North Business approach to business, it resulted in both success and significance for our company, and I believe it can do the same for yours. So, let's begin by defining each of these essentials, starting with core values.

Core Values

What are core values, anyway? Personally, I like Jim Collins and Jerry Porras's definition: "Core values are the organization's essential and enduring tenets—a small set of general guiding principles; not to be confused with specific cultural or operating practices; not to be compromised for financial gain or short-term expediency."[2]

Core values answer the question, "Who am I?"

Core values are discovered. They are not "set." They come from the founder of the organization, who then recruits, selects, hires, and onboards employees who hold the same core values.

So, the process to discover your core values is *not* figuring out what:

• Maximizes your wealth

---

2   Jim Collins and Jerry I. Porras, *Built to Last* (New York: HarperBusiness, 2011), 73.

- Sounds good to yourself or others
- Reflects your aspirations
- Complements your marketing campaign
- Pleases the financial community
- Looks attractive printed on glossy paper
- Echoes popular opinion
- Appeals to outsiders

Core values require:

- Authenticity
- Introspective reflection
- Articulating what is inside, bone deep
- Patience

I want to be a values-driven company that achieves results, not a results-driven company that has values.
—BOBBY ALBERT

In *The 7 Habits of Highly Effective People*, Stephen Covey explains that one important characteristic of proactive people is that they respond according to their values.[3] Covey's point is that when people know their personal core values, they make better life decisions. That, of course, spills over into making better business decisions.

3   See "Habit 1: Be Proactive" in Stephen R. Covey, *The 7 Habits of Highly Effective People* (New York: Simon & Schuster, 1989), 72, 80, 88, 106.

Take a True North Bearing

Do you know your core values? If so, what role do they play in your decisions? If not, do you find it difficult to identify an unchanging basis for your decision making?

Discover Your Core Values

In *Principled Profits*, I explain in detail how to discover your core values, but let me summarize it for you here.

First of all, finding your core values is a *process*, not an event. In fact, it took me two and a half years to discover my core values—but I didn't have the simplified roadmap I'm sharing with you.

Personally, I began by simply reflecting on my life, all the way back to when I was a little boy. While I was bicycling, taking long walks, or sitting in my "thinking chair," I asked myself questions like

- What do I stand for?
- What am I all about?

Then my antenna was up, and I asked myself deeper questions like

- Why did I say what I just said?
- Why was it important for me to say it that way?
- Why did I do what I just did?
- Why was it important for me to do it that way?

Next, I started to reflect on my past by asking questions like

- Who, even from an early age, influenced what I said and did?
- When did they influence me?
- Where did they influence me?
- How was I affected by these influences?

I was beginning to see some characteristics and behaviors in myself that I could trace back to my childhood, such as a thirst for learning, a focus on honesty, a desire to make the right decision regardless of the consequences, a need to lift others up, a determination to always perform to the best of my ability, a tendency to prioritize people above things, and a desire to positively impact the lives of others.

I was making progress, but I still had not fully and completely discovered who I was.

Finally, the day came. I don't know how to explain it, but I finally had enough clarity to discover who I was. To do that, I asked myself these two questions:

1. What things stir up my passion, get me excited, and give me energy? I wrote my answers on the left side of the page.
2. What things, when left undone, make me angry, frustrated, upset, and even foaming at the mouth? I wrote my answers on the right side of the page.

The entire page contained about thirty words.

As I continued to think about these questions and reviewed the two lists, I realized there were similar words on both sides of the page. I circled the matching words and came up with six:

1. Personal growth
2. Integrity
3. Add value
4. Excellence
5. Relationships
6. Significance

It hit me: this was "who I am"! And I was only able to know this for certain after spending several months thinking and reflecting on a variety of questions.

Now, it's your turn. I invite you to start the process of reflecting on your life. At TNB-book.com, you can download a copy of the Core Values Discovery Guide, which includes similar questions to the ones I list above, as well as the Core Values Validator Worksheet to make sure the values you've chosen are real, true, and authentic to you.

WARNING: *Do not* skip the process and only answer the last two questions of the Core Values Discovery Guide. Only completing part of the reflection process, or skipping it entirely, may produce quick results, but you're likely to end up with core values that are aspirational rather than authentic. In other words, you'll end up with who you *want* to be, rather than who you *are*—which are the wrong results. In fact, if you were a leader consulting with me, I would not give you the last two questions until you had spent perhaps a couple of months thinking on and praying over the first list of questions.

Once you discover your core values as a leader, you'll want to infuse them into your organization (if it doesn't reflect your core values already). For a practical process to introduce your core values to your company, see *Principled Profits*, part IV, "Core Values."

Now that we've reviewed the important process of determining your core values, let's move on to the next essential in True North Business: your purpose.

Purpose

Back in the early 1990s, the terms *purpose* and *mission* became very popular. The problem was that I'd find people interchanging these terms in articles and often in the same sentence.

The results were *confusion* and *frustration*!

I took it upon myself to look up the true definition of each of these terms. Of course, this was well before Google's search engine, so I had to thumb through physical copies of books to figure out the difference between them.

Once again, I believe Collins and Porras give the best definition of purpose in their book *Built to Last*: "The organization's fundamental reasons for existence beyond just making money."[4]

Your purpose answers the question, "Why do I exist?"

Okay, I now understood what a purpose was. How about mission?

The dictionary defined *mission statement* as "a formal summary of the aims and values of a company, organization, or individual."

More confusion and more frustration!

In practice, I found that businesses seemed to use the terms *purpose* and *mission* interchangeably, while nonprofits seemed to use the term *mission*. Even so, I have found almost all mission or purpose statements to be

- Too long and wordy, such that people cannot remember what it says or means
- Too generic, trying to be all things to all people
- Too technical

Even more confusion—and more frustration!

I felt I needed to draw a line in the sand to eliminate ambiguity between the terms *purpose* and *mission*, by creating a third term: *super-objective*.

I recommend businesses have a *purpose* (using Collins and Porras's definition above) and one or more super-objectives, which are the bridge between your core values/purpose/vision and your strategies/tactics/goals (more on super-objectives below).

I recommend nonprofits have a mission statement, as that term seems well established in that sector.

If you do use a mission statement, the best mission statements have the following qualities:

---

4   Jim Collins and Jerry I. Porras, *Built to Last* (New York: HarperBusiness, 2011), 73.

- *Clear.* Anyone can understand it.
- *Concise.* It is short, and it can be said in one breath.
- *Compelling.* It makes people want to say it again because it is delightful to hear. It begins with the words, "Every day . . ."
- *Catalytic.* Rather than just define what you successfully do, it encourages people to act, and it is achievable.
- *Contextual.* It describes coming from an actual circumstance and going to a new circumstance, and it must be measurable once it is practiced.

When a leader of either a business or nonprofit chooses to use a mission statement, I recommend that they . . .

- Also have a purpose that states why they exist, per definition above
- Make sure their mission statement is contextual, describing how they are "coming from an actual circumstance and going to a new circumstance"

Take a True North Bearing

Does your organization have a purpose statement, mission statement, or both? Are they clear, concise, and known by all team members?

Whether you choose to use a mission statement or not, we'll talk in much more detail about creating your purpose for your personal life and for your organization in part 3, "WOW!"

Vision

The term *vision* is a little more straightforward. We've all heard the term *vision statement*. But, what exactly is it?

Your vision is the future that you, as the leader, envision for your organization. It answers the question, "Where am I going?"

Your vision answers the question, "Where am I going?"

Where will you be in five years? Or ten or even thirty years?

Of course, no matter how hard you search, no one can answer that question with absolute certainty. But, I am certain of this: the journey toward your destiny always begins with a vision. And a vision is the roadmap to your destiny, the picture of your envisioned future. Without it, you may find yourself off course— or worse, going nowhere.

So, dream big . . . bigger . . . even bigger—because your dream will define the life you live.

Take a True North Bearing

Is your big, grand dream captured in a vision statement?
How well have you communicated it to your team?

We'll talk in much more detail about creating your vision statement for yourself and your organization in part 3, "WOW!"

Super-Objectives

Now, let's get back to super-objectives.

One day, on a long bicycle ride, I found myself asking, "At the end of the day, what do we want to accomplish in our business? And could this aim be stated simply so that our people could easily understand and remember it?"

I realized that, bottom line, we wanted to accomplish only two things:

1. Delight customers
2. Increase operating profits

I called these our *super-objectives* because they became the two high-level, overarching objectives for our business. They provided the bridge between our core values, purpose, and vision and our strategies, tactics, and goals—our drive for results.

Even though, in our company, every employee had an individually assigned role and responsibility, all of our employees had the same super-objectives. Every day our people clearly understood what they were to accomplish.

I did not find any other company that used the term *super-objectives*. It appears to be unique to the Albert Companies, and it became one of our True North Business Essentials.

Not long ago, a colleague told me that super-objective is a known term—in the theater. Wikibooks has defined a super-objective as a character's broad, overall objective that stays consistent throughout the play and provides a through line and arc for the character. It helps the actor solidify the motivations behind the character's actions and emotions. Some examples of super-objectives might be love, power, security, peace, finding purpose for your life, or having a family.

Because a need is stronger than a want, a need is usually a stronger choice for a character's super-objective because it creates more drive.

I found that interesting because it largely aligns with our definition of super-objectives in business, with one important difference: in theater, each character has a different super-objective, but in an organization, everyone has the same ones.

Take a True North Bearing

Have you ever asked yourself, "At the end of the day, what do we want to accomplish in our business?" How would you answer that question?

Just like core values, purpose, and vision apply to both organizations and individuals, super-objectives do, too. Individuals can ask themselves how well they've done on their super-objectives, just like the company can.

So, here are the four essentials we've covered so far:

1. Your core values describe *who* you are.
2. Your purpose is *why* you (or your organization) exist. You can think of your core values and your purpose together as your compass, your unchanging reference point.
3. Your vision is *where* you're headed.
4. Your super-objectives are *what* you're going to accomplish every day. To follow the True North metaphor, it might be how many miles you plan to hike each day.

However, you can have the most accurate compass (or GPS, if you prefer) and the most noble destination in the world, but if you don't know the right path, you'll never get there.

That leads us to the fifth True North essential: effective leadership.

CHAPTER 2

The Path of Effective Leadership

Improve How You Lead and Advance Where You Lead

Everything rises and falls on leadership.
—John C. Maxwell

Effective leadership is the path of your True North Business journey. It's the process by which your core values, purpose, vision, and super-objectives come alive.

Effective leadership includes the following five concepts:

1. Leading and managing
2. Relationships and results
3. Process and content
4. Principles vs. expediency
5. Goals and controls

If you'd like to learn more about any of these concepts, see parts I through VI of *Principled Profits*, but I'll summarize them for you here.

Leading and Managing

Many people use the terms *leading* and *managing* interchangeably. However, I have discovered most people have a "bent" toward either leading or managing. To find out whether your bent is toward leading or managing, visit www.BobbyAlbert.com/LeadershipIdentity to access my Leadership Identity Assessment. It takes just a few minutes to complete and you'll receive customized feedback when you complete the online assessment.

In fact, for the best results (both from the assessment and the impact of this section), I'd recommend you *not* read any further until you take five minutes and complete this assessment.

Have you completed it? Okay, let's continue.

I believe leading and managing are actually very different. To me, leaders focus on people, while managers focus on things.

Leaders	Managers
Seek input from others who may have additional insights or different views	Make decisions based on their own high levels of knowledge and experience
Guide engineers to seek predesign advice from teams of customers, prospects, and employees from other departments	Oversee engineers in designing a product that works well, but may be difficult to build, service, or repair, and may not reflect the changing interests of customers and prospects
Openly provide employees with information of potential interest regarding all aspects of the organization, in order to enhance their overall awareness and sense of belonging	Provide employees with information on a "need to know" basis
Interview prospective employees about what they have done, and ask extensive follow-up questions about how and why, to gain insights about their core values and style	Interview prospective employees primarily about their credentials, skills, and abilities

Take a True North Bearing

What is your bent? Do you lean more toward leading or managing? How did the Leadership Identity Assessment confirm or challenge what you already thought?

Regardless of your bent, effective leadership requires both leading *and* managing. In *Built to Last*, Collins and Porras call it the "genius of the AND":

> *Instead of being oppressed by the "Tyranny of the OR," highly visionary companies liberate themselves with the "Genius of the AND" . . . Instead of choosing between A OR B, they figure out a way to have both A AND B."*

They went on to say that this was not about "balance," in which you go fifty-fifty. Instead, highly visionary companies accomplish both at the same time, all the time.

For example, I've always known I had a bent toward leadership and investing in people. However, as an effective leader, I had to learn to wear two hats: when I had to make recruiting decisions, I put on my "leader" hat. When I had to review financial reports, I put on my "manager" hat. At the same time, I also learned to hire great managers so I could focus more on my own leadership gifts and strengths. That's the genius of the AND: leading *and* managing.

Relationships and Results

I have observed and learned over the years that the most effective leaders never lose sight of the fundamental importance of overseeing their team's drive for results. They need to be good at analyzing, planning, prioritizing, deciding, initiating, and following through on commitments.

So, if we need to focus on results, should we do so at the expense of relationships? No, I have learned that it is not an either-or situation. It's another case of the genius of the AND. Focusing on both relationships *and* results multiplies your effectiveness.

Let me show you what I mean. As I began to develop my leadership, I coined the term *Effectiveness Quotient* to describe or rate a person's level of effectiveness, following this both/and way of thinking.

To determine a leader's Effectiveness Quotient, you would first rate a leader's focus and drive as they relate to results on a scale from one to ten. Then you would rate the leader's focus and intention related to building and maintaining relationships, also on a scale from one to ten. This leader's Effectiveness Quotient would be the results rating times the relationship rating. So, a person with a results rating of six and a relationship rating of three would have an Effectiveness Quotient of eighteen.

I have found that it's not unusual for leaders to rate pretty well on results and fairly low on relationships.

Effectiveness Quotient

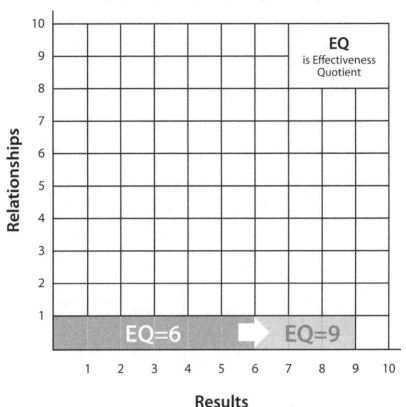

Look at the lower-left rectangle on the graph above. It represents the effectiveness of someone who reaches a six on the results scale (about average) and a one on the relationship scale (very low).

This person would focus on the bottom line and the end results of his work. Also, it's fair to say that he probably doesn't care much about building and enhancing relationships.

Even for those whose effectiveness is represented by the smallest shaded area on the graph, hope is not lost. They have some options to increase their level of effectiveness.

The first option is to, perhaps, work diligently to increase the drive for better results. The goal would be to raise that six to a nine. If this person worked individually and drove others with great intensity to achieve this, his Effectiveness Quotient would have increased by only 50 percent, and there would probably be "dead bodies" lying around. There'd be better results, but at the expense of the majority of this person's relationships—both professional and personal.

The second option is for this person to strive to increase his people skills and level of relationships. You might be thinking, "Bobby, if I take time to focus on developing people and relationships in my business, won't my results suffer?" That's a good question. Again, it is not an either-or situation. Let's look at the second Effectiveness Quotient graph.

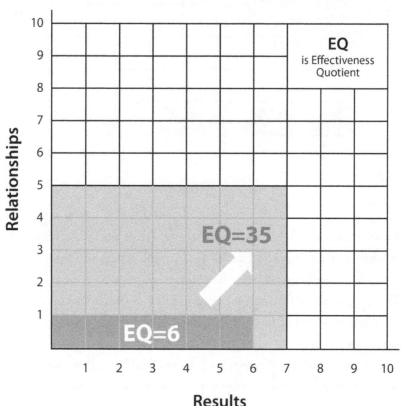

Suppose, through some personal development, the leader now raises his relationship skills from one to five. In my experience and observations, the level of the leader's results will also increase, possibly from six to seven, with no added intentional effort in that area. The total Effectiveness Quotient will now be thirty-five. The leader will have exponentially increased his original effectiveness of six by 583 percent, simply by focusing on the relationship part of leadership.

When you enhance relationships as you drive for results, your effectiveness increases exponentially.

Take a True North Bearing

Where is your focus? Is it on relationships or results? How would you rate your effectiveness?

Most leaders, while intelligent and well-meaning, tend to drive for results. They tell their subordinates the results they want, with little or no input from their subordinates. These managers don't realize that investing in relationships actually helps achieve significantly better results.

A relationship-oriented leadership style prepares the employees for the twists and turns along the path as they serve customers, suppliers (yes, even suppliers), and each other.

Employees who feel valued are much more willing to go the extra mile when those twists and turns happen—and they always happen.

Treat an employee like a robot, however, and watch production and satisfaction plummet. Instead of taking ownership and trying to solve problems, employees, feeling overwhelmed and disregarded, will shift blame and responsibilities to others.

The Path of Effective Leadership includes both relationships *and* results.

Process and Content

Another key part of effective leadership is the importance of what I call process and content. As a leader, I needed to focus equally on the content of *what* I said and did, and the process of *how* I said and did it.

When content is our main concern

- We drive for results.
- We focus on things.
- We manage things.
- We concentrate on what we say and do.

When process is our main concern

- We focus on how we communicate and interact with people on a day-to-day basis.
- We lead people.
- We concentrate on how we set and pursue our goals (how we do something).

Obviously, content is crucial for effective leadership. Without clear, well-communicated, meaningful, and attainable objectives, people are directionless. They need to know where you expect them to go.

On the other hand, process is just as important. How we say or do something can powerfully impact how someone receives our message. Our body language and tone of voice, for example, may either reinforce or contradict what we're saying. With process, we're focused on people—leading them, enhancing relationships, and intentionally monitoring how we say and do things. It also includes communication (for mutual understanding), coordination (to coordinate interactions), and cooperation (with a spirit of mutual support and assistance).

Take a True North Bearing

Do you concentrate more on what you say and do or how you say and do things? Would you consider giving special attention to how you say and do things? What do you have to lose? What might you gain from this approach?

Principle vs. Expediency

Even if we're focusing on leading and managing, relationships and results, and process and content, we may still find ourselves wandering away from the Path of Effective Leadership. How? When we're under stress, we may be doing what's *expedient* rather than following trusted leadership *principles*—without even realizing it.

When we're under stress, we can find ourselves in reactive mode, where we tend to make expedient decisions that are more convenient and popular, rather than principled decisions. In other words, we tend to do what's easiest and quickest or what makes us the happiest in the short run. At the same time, we worry more about protecting our rights instead of serving others. Deep down, expedient behavior is most often rooted in unhealthy fears. Such behavior eventually leads to undesirable results and negative consequences. And it will certainly lead to poor business outcomes.

Take a True North Bearing

Have you been in reactive mode lately? What have you experienced when you behave in an expedient way?

With principled behavior, however, we begin to work on the things we can do something about. By working on ourselves instead of worrying about conditions, we are even able to influence the conditions.

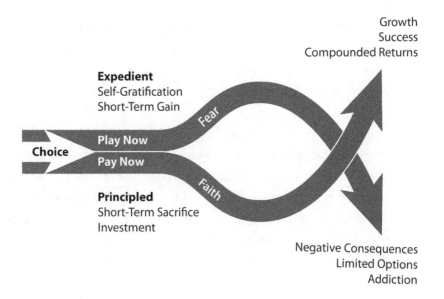

If you're on the Path of Effective Leadership, you know that if you really want to improve your situation, the most positive way you can do that is to work on the one thing over which you have control—*you*.

Instead of an outside-in paradigm that tells us what's out there has to change before we can change, we have an inside-out paradigm that tells us we can have an effective positive change on what's out there by working on *being who we are*. We're willing to do things emotion-driven people will not bother to do, and as a result, we enjoy long-term success.

Take a True North Bearing

What are you more likely to do: play now and pay later—or pay now and play later? After viewing the diagram above, do the benefits and consequences become clearer?

Would you give me permission to ask you some questions to further explore whether expediency might be affecting your leadership?

If the weather is good, do you feel good? If it isn't, does it affect your attitude and your performance?

When people treat you well, do you feel well? When people don't, do you become defensive or protective? Do your emotions change based on the behavior of others?

Are your feelings driven by circumstances, by conditions, or by your environment?

Do you react to changes and challenges by saying things like

- It's in my DNA. I inherited it from past generations.
- It's my parents' fault. I was raised that way.
- It's my boss's fault.
- It's my spouse's fault.
- It's the government's fault.
- It's the economy.

In other words, do you believe someone or something in your environment is responsible for your current situation, personal tendencies, or character? Do you feel increasingly victimized and out of control, not in charge of your life or your destiny?

> *Any time you think the problem is out there, that very thought is the problem.*
> —STEPHEN R. COVEY

If you're not sure of your answers to the above questions, your language can also be a strong indicator of the degree to which you react to your external situation and let your feelings and emotions dominate your response and absolve you of responsibility. Take a look at the following chart and consider how often you use this kind of reactive language versus the more responsible alternative.

Reactive Language	Underlying Belief	Responsible Alternative
"That's just the way I am."	There is nothing I can do about it.	Let me look into my options.
"I can't do that."	Something outside me is limiting me.	I am choosing not to do that.
"I just don't have time."	Something outside me is controlling my priorities.	Let me see where I can schedule time into my calendar.
"My boss makes me so mad."	My emotional life is governed by someone outside my control.	I need to ask my boss for some time to talk through this thing that frustrates me.
"I have to do it."	Circumstances or other people are forcing me to do it.	I am choosing to do it.

The whole spirit of the comments in the first column above is a transfer of responsibility to someone or something else to take care of us as we react based on our feelings and emotions. We are giving up our personal responsibility by empowering other people, conditions, and circumstances to control us.

So, we blame; we use accusing attitudes and reactive, emotion-driven language; and we incur increasing feelings of victimization for our own stagnant situation. The result is expedient leadership, which wreaks havoc in our lives, mentally, emotionally, spiritually, and physically. If we've given up leading ourselves, how can we effectively lead others?

Take a True North Bearing

Is there one decision that you're considering today that you can approach in a more principled way? How so?

Another way expediency shows up is in your mindset. Expedient behavior tends to go hand in hand with what's known as a *scarcity mindset*.

People with a scarcity mindset see their glass as half-empty. They focus on their deficiencies rather than their gifts, and they always feel that their commodities are about to run out. Consequently, people with a scarcity mindset tend to be protective of what they have and what they know. They also tend to focus on short-term gain and function in reactive mode, which typically results in more expedient behavior.

The opposite of a scarcity mindset is an *abundance mindset*, and it goes hand in hand with principled behavior. People with an abundance mindset see their glass as half-full. They believe that today's short-term pain, sacrifice, and investment in time, energy, and money will eventually bring long-term growth, blessings, and success.

People with an abundance mindset view their resources as a farmer views seeds. A successful farmer liberally sows seeds, trying to ensure a good fall harvest.

He believes in the principle of sowing and reaping. The more he sows, the more he reaps.

You can't harvest what you haven't planted.

Similarly, effective leaders and people with an abundance mindset see their resources as sufficient and plentiful seeds to be sown. They know the harvest will come and more will be created.

Take a True North Bearing

Do you have a scarcity mindset? Or do you have an abundance mindset?

Effective leadership is principled leadership. When you realize you're overstressed, making expedient decisions, and operating from a scarcity mindset, take a moment to remind yourself of the principles of True North Business: your core values, your purpose, your vision, your super-objectives, and these five key concepts of effective leadership.

Goals and Controls

The final part of effective leadership is what I call *goals and controls*. Effective leaders, as well as highly motivated employees who form a high-performance team and have a can-do spirit, will continually revisit two questions:

1. What is our *goal*?
2. Are we making progress toward it (*controls*)?

Goals

The goals of individuals and the group must be clearly defined, understood, and—to be fully beneficial—accepted as reasonable. The following characteristics are indicative of a clear goal:

- Specific
- Vital
- Measurable
- Achievable
- Challenging
- Time-bound

In an organization, it is the leader's responsibility to clarify and communicate what a goal is. Just like the terms *purpose* and *vision*, I often find that the word *goal* is used loosely in an organization to mean different things to different people at different times and under different circumstances. This vagueness only adds to the confusion.

> *All good performance starts with clear goals.*
> —KEN BLANCHARD

To that end, all leaders can set and achieve high-performance goals by following this four-step process:

1. Ask
2. Connect
3. Analyze
4. Clarify

Ask. At the very beginning of the goal-setting process and before defining any team or company goals, ask key employees for input. To determine who to ask, consider the following questions:

- Who can help me set a better goal?
- Who will have to carry it out?
- Who will be impacted by it?

Once you determine who to ask, gather input from these team members. Consider the following questions:

- Where have we been?
- Where are we now?
- Where are we going?

Connect. The next step in setting goals is to connect with your people. One of the best ways to connect with your people is to regularly do Management By Walking Around (MBWA).

MBWA is an unstructured manner of walking or wandering through the workplace to talk with employees or inquire about the status of ongoing work. It should be done by you, as the leader, as well as your leadership team so that everyone knows with certainty what your employees are thinking and what is working and not working, from their perspective.

And, just as important, you want to learn the following:

- What do your customers want to buy from you?
- How can/does your organization give your customers what they want?

If you ask questions and listen, the responses will be amazing. People will become energized simply because you asked.

Analyze. The next step is to do a SWOT analysis, which stands for *strengths*, *weaknesses*, *opportunities*, and *threats*. A SWOT analysis is a structured planning method used to find your competitive advantage by evaluating the internal factors and external factors affecting the organization.

To assess your organization's internal factors, write down the following:

- *Strengths.* These are the characteristics of the business or project that give it an advantage over others.
- *Weaknesses.* These are the characteristics that place the business or project at a disadvantage relative to others.

To assess your organization's external factors, write down the following:

- *Opportunities.* These are the elements that the project could exploit to its advantage.
- *Threats.* These are the elements in the environment that could cause trouble for the business or project.

External factors may include macroeconomic matters, technological changes, legislation, and sociocultural changes, as well as changes in the marketplace (customers and suppliers) or in competitive position.

Tip: Become a student of specific and general industry and market trends.

Clarify. Now that you have gathered all the input you need, the final step is to set your goals and regularly communicate them.

As the leader in my company, in addition to communicating our goals, I was also very intentional about clarifying and clearly communicating exactly what I meant when I used the term *goals*—I was only referring to *measurable* goals (see below). I regularly explained the difference between . . .

- Our True North Business Essentials:
  - » Core values: who are we?
  - » Purpose: why do we exist?
  - » Vision: where are we going?
  - » Super-objectives (or mission, for nonprofits): what do we want to accomplish every day?
- Strategic plans: what do we want to accomplish long term?

- Tactical plans:
  » How can we get there?
  » When do we want to arrive?
  » Who can make it happen on schedule?
- Measurable goals: what are the numeric and timeliness measures of success?

This formed the roadmap for our business, which you'll learn much more about in part 2.

Take a True North Bearing

As the leader of your business, can you answer this question: what are your goals? And are you making progress toward your goals?

Controls

Once the process of setting goals is complete, then the process of following up and following through on the goals should begin. This next stage requires controls that include these elements:

- Frequent and regular communication reporting on the progress of those tactical projects and goals.
- Intentional communication to ensure your people's progress on objectives and strategies is in alignment with your core values, purpose, vision, and super-objectives (or mission, for nonprofits).

One tool you can use to successfully achieve your goals and set up controls is a True North Business Review. This review is a monthly forum the purpose of which is to continually revisit two questions:

1. What are our goals?
2. Are we making progress (controls)?

If you'd like more information on how to start a monthly True North Business Review in your company, see TNB-book.com to download my "True North Business Review Quick-Start Guide."

The Roadmap of True North Business

Now that you understand the five essentials of True North Business, it's time to learn how to apply them to your organization. In part 2, we'll start with your roadmap to True North Business: the leadership practice of ON/IN.

PART TWO

ON/IN

CHAPTER 3

If You're Tired of Fighting Alligators, Drain the Swamp!

Address the Important to Conquer the Urgent

What is important is seldom urgent and what is urgent is seldom important.
—Dwight D. Eisenhower

The year was 1973, and life was good:

- I had just graduated with honors from our local state university after only three years and at the age of twenty.
- I had concluded serving as the president of student government (PSG) at a university of over four thousand students.
- During that academic year, I helped my fraternity win both the scholarship and intramural sports trophies.
- I was waiting to hear about my acceptance to law school.
- I became engaged to my future wife, with plans to wed in January 1974.

Life was indeed good—until late one summer evening when I was playing goalie in a game of foosball with my college buddies. One of my friends came up to me and said, "Bobby, we just got a call, and they said your dad has had a heart attack. They have taken him to the emergency room."

My friends hopped in the car with me, and we rushed to the emergency room. When I entered those double doors with my friends behind me, I found my mom seated in a chair to my left. Upon seeing me, she quickly got up. Then our long-time friend and family doctor walked up to both of us. Our eyes were riveted on his face, seeking answers to questions we were afraid to ask. He softly said, "I could not save him."

My mom and I were so shocked that neither one of us displayed any emotion. We were absolutely stunned. I felt as if all my energy had been completely drained from me. My mind kept telling me it wasn't true, that it was just a bad dream and I was going to wake up and everything was going to be OK.

My dad's death occurred on a Friday night. Since I had been working on the moving trucks of our family's moving company during the normal work week and since I usually came in on Saturday mornings to do some of Dad's bookkeeping and prepare paperwork for the upcoming week, I knew that somebody needed to make decisions about what we were going to do with the upcoming week's jobs.

That Friday night, I knew that "somebody" was me.

So, I did what leaders do. They step up to the plate, give directions, and act. Looking back, when I stepped up to the plate, it gave all our employees, and even my mom, a sense of confidence and a resolve that we were going to make it work. From that point forward, I did not pursue going to law school. I became the new leader of our small family business, which had only five employees.

Within days of my father's funeral, I paid a visit to my father's three bankers. I knew each of these men, having been around them since I was a little boy. Well, I was in for another shock. I discovered we were $70,000 in debt, and our total gross revenue was less than $90,000. Not good.

Financially, we were way upside down. Two of the bankers wanted to shut us down and sell the assets to pay off the debt. It was easy to see why:

- They held only one old, small moving van as collateral.

- They were looking at the very young twenty-year-old son who had never run a business before.
- Our business was so upside down that the chances of us ever pulling out of this financial crisis were slim to none.
- They knew from experience that when a son (or any second-generation family member) takes over the business, the likelihood of success is remote at best.
- They feared my motivations for wanting to give it a try were only sentimental (emotional) and not reasonable or prudent.

To my surprise, one of the bankers, who understood all the reasons why they should not give me a chance, somehow convinced the other two to give me a chance. However, they would not loan me any more money, and I would have to use the cash from the business to pay down the debt, pay operating expenses, and make enough to live on. Yikes!

The Challenge of Leadership

Immediately, I jumped in with both feet, devoting all of my ability, energy, and might to building the business. It was obvious we needed more revenue, and that was my main focus. I had to scrape and scrape and scrape to make it work. My wife still reminds me today that our weekly food budget was twenty dollars.

Take a True North Bearing

Have you ever had a season in your life when everything was going well, and then, suddenly, your world collapsed? How did you respond?

At our company, one of the first things I had to do was to sit down with our five employees and ask each of them to take a pay cut. Yes, you heard me correctly, a pay cut.

Those were the most difficult conversations I had ever experienced as a still-wet-behind-the-ears, twenty-year-old kid. I was shaking as I went into those conversations because I knew it was going affect my employees' ability to support their families.

To my surprise, all five employees accepted the change. I believe they accepted it out of respect for both my dad, because he really took care of his employees, and for me, because they had seen my work ethic firsthand on the moving trucks and at the storage warehouse since I was twelve years old. They knew I had always wanted to serve them, rather than be served.

Take a True North Bearing

Have you ever had an uncomfortable conversation with an employee? How did you handle it?

To pay down some of the debt, I even sold my personal car. My dad really did take good care of his employees, and he had furnished two employees with vehicles that were used in the business. I knew I could not ask them to give up those vehicles just because I was on foot. However, I did ask one of them, who drove right by my house, to pick me up in the morning and take me home in the evening. He agreed, and he did so for about two years.

Everyday Crisis Mode

For the next year and a half, I found myself working harder and harder IN the business. I was working seven days a week, always the first one to arrive (with the employee who gave me a ride) and the last one to leave, late at night (also with that employee).

As you can imagine, I was in crisis mode every day. I was constantly reacting to pressing problems, deadlines, phone calls, and projects. I wore many hats, doing hands-on work in every aspect of our business to save labor cost and applying "Band-Aids" to issues until I could get back to them. I was focused on tactical action steps, driving for results just to meet our daily and weekly needs.

As I began to lead our small company by day, I started fighting other problems by night. Worries plagued me like alligators trying to take me under. I was concerned about people, money/financing, government regulations, changing patterns of customer buying . . . the list was endless.

Specifically, I worried about these three issues:

1. Increasing revenue
2. Decreasing expenses
3. Increasing productivity

After just a year and a half, I was about to burn out—working seven days a week IN the business and reacting to its daily and weekly demands.

When dealing with all the worries threatening to pull me under, I had to remind myself that my initial objective wasn't to fight alligators, it was to drain the swamp.

Are You Part of the 85 Percent?

As a leader, owner, president, or CEO, do you feel as if you're up to your neck in alligators? Do you feel like a concrete block has been tied to your ankles, pulling down even your best efforts? Does it seem like your results don't reflect your hard work? Do you wonder if you are a failure? I can assure you that you are not alone in your season of "troubled waters."

As I have mentored struggling leaders, departmental managers, owners, presidents, CEOs, and other C-level executives, I've found that 85 percent of them are working harder and harder IN the business. They're focused on the tactical action steps required to run the business on a daily, weekly, and monthly basis, just like I used to be.

That means only 15 percent of leaders are focused on the overarching guiding beliefs and plans of their organization, things like their core values, purpose, vision, super-objectives, and strategic plans.

Well, you no longer need to feel like you're sinking in an ocean of despair. Instead of working harder and harder IN your business, there is a better way! A different approach allowed me to rise above the choppy waters and achieve better results for myself and my company.

The ON/IN Leadership Practice

Fortunately, I discovered how to drain the swamp by learning to work ON the business, not just IN the business. I learned to create an environment where alligators could not survive and threaten my leadership and my business. It's what kept me aware of my True North and headed toward my envisioned future–all the years I was in business and beyond.

I started working proactively (my natural bent prior to my dad's death) rather than reactively. I began to pause from my day-to-day work activity for reflection, planning, and preparation.

Within a couple of years after taking this proactive approach to our business by working ON the business, not just IN the business, we experienced triple-digit growth, and we had the highest amount of profits in the history of our company. We kept employing this approach year after year and eventually grew our fledgling company to an organization with over one hundred fifty employees.

Over time, I began to call this simple approach the ON/IN (pronounced "on and in") leadership practice:

Work ON the business while we work IN the business.

The good news is that any leader can tap the power of the ON/IN practice to grow his business.

So, what exactly does it mean to work ON the business while we work IN the business? You've heard the old saying, "Don't just sit there, do something." That's a good description of what it means to work IN the business. You're focused on tactics, achieving results, serving customers, and doing what needs to be done.

Well, when you work ON the business, the saying should be, "Don't just do something, sit there." But don't sit idly! Plan what is to be accomplished, by when, and what needs to be done along the way so that when you get back to working IN the business, you've chosen the right tactics to achieve the results you want.

Distance racers learn they can start off too fast in a race if they don't have a plan and pace themselves. Mountain climbers know it's not good enough to reach the top; if they haven't allowed enough time and provisions for climbing down, they'll die. Underwater divers must plan what to do and when to return to the surface—or they, too, will die. And, as a True North Business leader, your first task is to plan your journey with the pace, time, and provisions you need for an optimal outcome.

It's another paradox: to achieve greater levels of success, you need to spend less time working IN the business and make regular time to work ON the business.

Take a True North Bearing

What percentage of your time are you working IN your business? What percentage of your time are you working ON your business?

The Greatest Leadership Gap

"Bobby, I want you to come in and fix my people." As I have mentored CEOs, presidents, owners, and other key leaders, this is the most common initial request that I hear.

What about you? Do you ever want someone to come in and "fix" your people? Have you ever looked in the mirror and thought, "If only someone would come in and fix my employees?" Take another serious look in the mirror. Can I suggest that your people are merely a reflection of you?

Would you give me permission to speak truth to you? Fellow leader, *you* are the one who needs to be "fixed."

Everything rises and falls on leadership.
—JOHN MAXWELL

In *The 21 Irrefutable Laws of Leadership*, John Maxwell explains The Law of Magnetism—Who You Are Is Who You Attract. He goes on to say, "If you want to attract better people, become the kind of person you desire to attract."[5]

Maxwell nailed the problem of personal growth with a quote from Dick Biggs: "The greatest gap in the world is the one between knowing and doing."[6]

I have observed the following to be true as well:

- The greatest *leadership* gap in the world is understanding the difference between what you "want" and what you "need."
- All leaders can achieve what they have always "wanted" by changing how they think about what they "need."

The following chart details the differences between needs and wants.

	Needs	Wants
Definition	Something you must fulfill to survive	Something you emotionally wish to have or a choice you'd like to make
Permanence	Principles: Do not change with time	Preferences: Might change over time
If Unfulfilled	Leader/organization will suffer	Leader/organization will continue in the same direction
Universality	Leaders/organizations all have the same needs	Leaders/organizations have different wants

5   John Maxwell, *The 21 Irrefutable Laws of Leadership: Follow Them and People Will Follow You* (Nashville: Thomas Nelson, 2007).

6   John Maxwell, "Are You Driven by Character or Emotion?" (blog post), April 11, 2014, http://blog.johnmaxwell.com/blog/are-you-driven-by-character-or-emotion.

Needs and wants are separate forces that compel action for satisfaction. Needs are principles that, if not met on time, put the survival of the leader or organization at stake. In contrast, wants are something the leader craves, but wants do not challenge the leader/organization's survival if not satisfied.

Needs can be distinguished from wants based on their level of importance. Needs are of the utmost importance. However, a leader will often contend that his wants are of immense importance, even though he may or may not be realistically able to obtain them.

At the beginning of *The Wizard of Oz*, Dorothy wants out of Kansas. She wants to be in a more exciting place. By the end, she realizes that she needs to be surrounded by her family and friends.

At the beginning of *Star Wars Episode IV*, Luke wants adventure and something external. By the end, he realizes that what he needs is trust (in himself, others, and the Force), which is something internal.

Do you want to grow your business? Do you want to achieve successful results like you have never seen before? Then the first person you need to work ON is staring you in the mirror each morning.

The Leadership Paradox: Most leaders believe their first job is to grow their business. The truth is, you need to grow yourself first.

The ON/IN practice is what each of us needs. When you work ON the business, you take time to remove yourself from the daily grind of working IN the business. This enables you to think about things on a higher level and make intentional plans about your life and business.

Thinking for a Change

One of the reasons people don't achieve their dreams is that they desire to change their results without changing their thinking.
—JOHN MAXWELL

As the leader, your ability to achieve what you have always wanted requires you to change how you think by applying the ON/IN practice. The change process starts with understanding that everything begins with a thought.

When you change what you think, you change what you do, and change who you are.

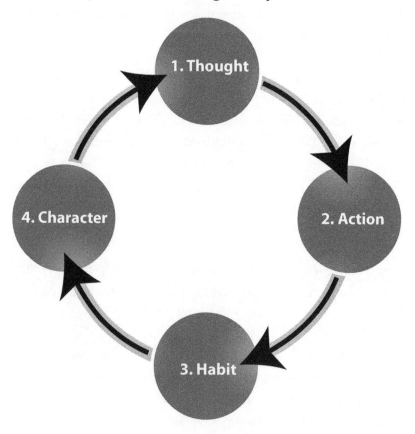

When you change how you think, and you act on that new thinking for thirty to sixty days, you will develop a habit, which eventually shapes who you are, your character. Once you embrace "thinking for a change," you will discover why . . .

Unsuccessful people don't think like
successful people do.

I believe you, as the leader, are now ready to get working ON, not just IN, the business. Let's first fix you, then focus on your people, and finally, you will be able to turn your attention toward your business.

Take a True North Bearing

Have you been looking in the mirror? What do you see? Do you see the reflection of your people in you?

What's Your Leadership Roadmap?

Years ago, after losing more than fifty pounds of weight in six months, I participated in a short bicycle race. It was a fifteen-mile, individual time trial, a race where each individual competes against the clock. To my surprise, I was leading the race . . . until close to the finish line when I turned down the wrong road, one with a dead end.

When you are the leader of the pack, make sure you have
a roadmap so you don't race down a dead-end street.

If you want to lead well, you'll use proactive planning to make informed decisions. If you don't, you'll lead your people into a dead-end situation, with no options and probable failure.

I'd like to share with you the roadmap for my business, which I call the Values-Driven Organizational Hierarchy. I have spent about twenty years refining this diagram. I've added to it, subtracted from it, changed the look, and changed the wording, all to reflect new insights and incorporate the helpful feedback I've received from others.

Values-Driven Organizational Hierarchy

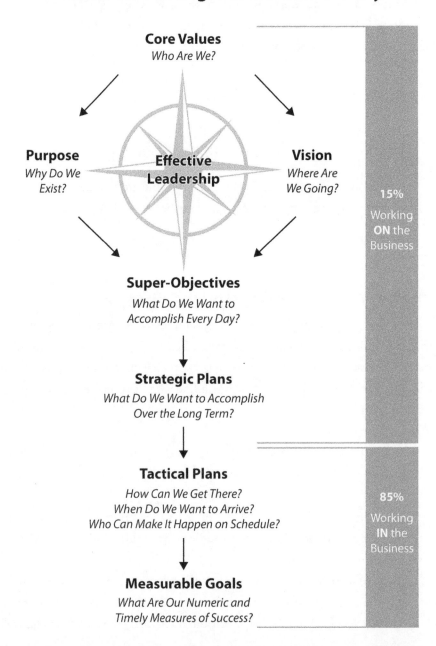

You can also download a free copy of my Values-Driven Organizational Hierarchy at TNB-book.com.

I have used this roadmap to show our employees how independent each element of our business is and, at the same time, how interdependent all the elements are in relationship to each other. It's a summary of how everything you'll learn in this book comes together in a single journey. It's your True North roadmap to long-term business success.

As you see from the diagram, working ON the business includes identifying your core values, purpose, vision, and super-objectives, as well as planning your strategies, tactics, and measurable goals.

Working IN your business includes executing the tactics and measurable goals you've planned. It's just one small part of the roadmap, yet it's where 85 percent of us spend nearly 100 percent of our time.

In addition to what's listed on the diagram, working ON your business also includes constantly searching for ways to improve the value you provide your customers and taking time to consider how your work could be done more *effectively* and *efficiently*. These two terms may sound similar, but they're actually quite different.

Effectiveness means doing the right thing, which will determine your success. A person's or group's effectiveness is the extent to which their purpose, vision, super-objectives, strategies, tactics, and measurable goals are completed. In other words, have the targeted results been achieved?

Efficiency, on the other hand, means doing things right, which will determine your survival. Efficiency is the extent to which results have been achieved with minimal use of available resources (labor, equipment, materials, etc.).

Having a roadmap for working ON, not just IN, the business helps you, as the leader. And, most of all, your employees will know not only *where* the organization is going and why but also *how* they will get there. This understanding enables your organization to become more effective and efficient long term.

The ultimate evidence of the success of such efforts is your ability to profitably achieve customer delight—giving a customer what I call a Triple-E: an *experience* that *exceeds* their *expectations.*

Take a True North Bearing

Do you have a roadmap for your business? Do you spend time working ON your business, or are you too busy working IN your business?

Work ON the Business

Now that you have a roadmap, how do you begin using the ON/IN leadership practice in your business? At a high level, it involves employing a three-prong strategy:

1. Grow yourself.
2. Grow your people.
3. Grow your business.

That's exactly what you'll learn to do in the following chapters, and it all starts with growing yourself.

CHAPTER 4

Grow Yourself

Focus on the Leader in Your Mirror

You cannot change your destination overnight, but you can change your direction overnight. If you want to reach your goals and fulfill your potential, become intentional about your personal growth. It will change your life.
—JIM ROHN

When I was a little boy, I was full of curiosity. I was also full of energy. My parents could have said I had ADDDDDDDDDDD! I believe that is why they put me in kindergarten at the age of four, a year younger than most of the other kids.

Throughout all my early years in school, I struggled just to make average grades (and sometimes below-average grades). During the spring of fifth grade, I made an F in science on my six-week report card. I tried to explain to my parents that I did not even remember us studying science that six weeks (a belief I still hold today). If I could not remember studying science in the first place, that may explain why I made an F!

One late afternoon before the last six weeks of that spring semester, my dad and I were playing catch with a baseball in the backyard, and he gently remarked, "Bobby, how about you see what you can do the last six weeks." Until then, I'd been satisfied with my so-so to average grades. But his simple challenge really took hold of me.

From that day forward, until the end of the school year, I worked toward making the best grades I could achieve. When I received my grades for that last six weeks, I was surprised by how well I did. My parents were even shocked.

That was the first time I realized my true personal growth potential. Until that moment, I'd never taken the time to ponder what I wanted to achieve. I had worked to get the job done quickly so I could be released to play. I worked IN school, not ON school.

Ever since that fifth-grade moment, my grades were always at the top of the class, all the way through college. I committed to becoming a lifelong learner, and even after all these years, I still read and study two to three hours a day.

When you work ON your business, you take time to remove yourself from the daily grind of working IN the business. This enables you to think about things on a higher level and make intentional plans about your life and business.

Most leaders believe their first job is to grow their business. The truth is, your first job is to grow YOU.

And if you really want to grow your business and achieve results you have never seen before, the first thing you need to work ON is staring you in the mirror each morning.

Take a True North Bearing

Are you a lifelong learner? Are you ready to first grow you?

Mason Jars and Business Growth

Recently, I arrived at a meeting to find an empty Mason jar positioned in front of each person sitting around the table. An orange balloon was lying beside each jar. The facilitator instructed each of us to put the balloon inside our jar and blow up the balloon until it filled the jar. Then we tied a knot at the tip of the balloon to prevent the air from escaping. After everyone finished, he shared the following story:

> *A pumpkin farmer was strolling through his rows of beautiful green leaves. At the beginning of the season, the acorn-size pumpkins were beginning to add dots to the landscape. When he glanced down, he noticed a clear glass jar and curiosity got the best of him.*
>
> *He brought the jar over to one of his pumpkin buds, slipped the small pumpkin inside, and left it sitting there in the field. Months later, with the experiment long forgotten, the farmer walked his land with great satisfaction as large, beautiful pumpkins covered the patch.*
>
> *Startled, he noticed the glass jar totally intact yet completely filled up with that little pumpkin that grew inside. It was hard not to notice how the thin glass barrier defined the shape of the orange mass within. The pumpkin was only one-third of the size it should have been.[7]*

The problem for this little pumpkin is the same problem for most businesses today. Rather than growing to their full potential, they conform to the limitations defined by their leader.

These "glass jars" create invisible impediments to growth and define the shape of the business's future. No one's thinking—neither your employees' nor your own—will ever get any bigger than the size of their "jar."

---

7   Will Mancini, *Church Unique: How Missional Leaders Cast Vision, Capture Culture, and Create Movement* (San Francisco: Jossey-Bass, 2008), 3-4.

The Myths of Personal Growth

You can't handle the truth!
—JACK NICHOLSON

Have you ever heard this iconic quote from the film *A Few Good Men*? It is true for so many leaders. I have often found leaders don't want to hear that they aren't growing personally or even that their people aren't growing.

Many leaders have settled for mediocrity. They have had opportunity after opportunity to accomplish great things, but, somehow, they've never achieved much. Some may feel regretful because they have gone so long without experiencing personal growth that they have now begun to feel they have missed out on life.

Why? Perhaps because they gave into the following myths of growth.

Myth 1. Growth is automatic.

Growth is not automatic. We think that our minds will just take care of themselves and keep growing, like our bodies did when we were younger.

However, we don't realize that our minds were growing in high school and college because we had someone pushing us to learn and improve. If you don't have a teacher or coach pushing you to become better, you'll need to step up and motivate yourself to grow.

Myth 2. Growth comes with experience.

Many people believe that personal growth simply results from experience. But, growth comes with experience *only if* you reflect upon what you have learned from both your successes and mistakes.

Experience isn't the best teacher—
evaluated experience is.
—JOHN MAXWELL

Myth 3. Growth comes from information.

Knowledge is not enough. I'm sure you've known people, like I have, full of information and data but doing nothing to apply all this wonderful knowledge to benefit themselves or others.

Most leaders feel their problem is their people, but . . .

Can you handle the truth?

The truth is, no matter what work you do or where you do it, your greatest challenge is *you*. No matter what you think your biggest problem is, your biggest problem is *you*.

Why? In *The 21 Irrefutable Laws of Leadership*, John Maxwell tells us that we are the "lids" on our own success. I have found this to be true—my own leadership skills are often the lid, or limiting variable, on my personal life and business success.

If your leadership skills are strong, the organization's lid is high. But, if your leadership is lacking, then the organization is limited. Using John Maxwell's terminology, you are the lid, or limiter, on the progress you desire. Your organization, your division, or your department will be contained by your leadership.

Your business is the size of you. Your employees will not grow beyond you. And if they do grow faster and greater than you, they will leave you to seek employment elsewhere.

Your perspective on life and in business will be limited by your own personal growth. You cannot grow your business until you grow your people. But, you will not grow your people until you first grow you. You cannot teach your family or your employees anything greater than what you know and have experienced.

Many leaders are looking for that quick fix to growth, but if you are not growing, you will be the lid on your organization's growth, no matter how many quick fixes you try.

The problem is not the size of your business. The problem is the size of you.

Take a True North Bearing

In what ways have you put your business inside of a Mason jar? What can you do to remove the limits on the size of your business? Are you willing to change and invest in personal growth for yourself and your people?

You, as the leader, can break the mold and smash your jar by working ON yourself first. Consequently, you will be able to expand your thinking to grow your people and your business.

The First Step

Recently, I read a famous story told by James Clear:

> *By 1918, Charles M. Schwab was one of the richest men in the world. Schwab was the president of the Bethlehem Steel Corporation, the largest shipbuilder and the second-largest steel producer in America at the time.*
>
> *The famous inventor Thomas Edison once referred to Schwab as the "master hustler." He was constantly seeking an edge over the competition.*
>
> *One day in 1918, in his quest to increase the efficiency of his team and discover better ways to get things done, Schwab arranged a meeting with a highly respected productivity consultant named Ivy Lee.*
>
> *Lee was a successful businessman in his own right and is widely remembered as a pioneer in the field of public relations. As the story*

goes, Schwab brought Lee into his office and said, "Show me a way to get more things done."

"Give me fifteen minutes with each of your executives," Lee replied.

"How much will it cost me?" Schwab asked.

"Nothing," Lee said, "unless it works. After three months, you can send me a check for whatever you feel it's worth to you."

During his fifteen minutes with each executive, Lee explained his simple method for achieving peak productivity:

1. *At the end of each work day, write down the six most important things you need to accomplish tomorrow. Do not write down more than six tasks.*
2. *Prioritize those six items in order of their true importance.*
3. *When you arrive tomorrow, concentrate only on the first task. Work until the first task is finished before moving on to the second task.*
4. *Approach the rest of your list in the same fashion. At the end of the day, move any unfinished items to a new list of six tasks for the following day.*
5. *Repeat this process every working day.*

The strategy sounded simple, but Schwab and his executive team at Bethlehem Steel gave it a try. After three months, Schwab was so delighted with the progress his company had made that he called Lee into his office and wrote him a check for $25,000.

A $25,000 check written in 1918 is the equivalent of a $400,000 check in 2015.[8]

---

8   James Clear, "The Ivy Lee Method: The Daily Routine Experts Recommend for Peak Productivity," https://jamesclear.com/ivy-lee, accessed May 30, 2018.

Over the last hundred years, our world has changed in every way imaginable, but this principle remains. Planning the next day in advance and working down your prioritized list with intention still yields tremendous results.

> *The secret of our success is found in our daily agenda.*
> —Tag Short

As part of working ON the business, I'd like to recommend that the first item of true importance on your daily list should be an area of personal growth. Grow yourself first.

Do you want to reach your full potential? Are you tired of merely experiencing life and hoping your people will acquire personal growth along the way?

You are not alone.

Remember, success is a journey, not a destination.

> *You cannot change your destination overnight, but you can change your direction overnight.*
> —Jim Rohn

If you really want to reach your potential and not just hope you will have personal growth along the way, you must go out of your way to seize personal growth opportunities as if your life depended on it. And it does. Not just your life, but the lives of your people and your business, too.

Without change, there can be no growth. You must commit yourself to not only accepting change, but seeking it.

Take a True North Bearing

Do you have a short daily task list? Do you prioritize your list? Do you include personal growth on your daily list?

Five Habits of Personal Growth

A few years ago, I took my oldest grandson to a traditional circus passing through our hometown. We had such a great time. When I was a little boy, my dad would take me to the circus, and I have such fond memories of those days. Of course, when our three boys were young, I took them as well.

I have always been amazed by the overwhelming size and raw power of the elephants. How can these enormous animals be held by a simple chain they could easily break?

It turns out that when an elephant is born into captivity, it is chained to a post that prevents it from escaping. Early on, infant elephants test, again and again, the chain that binds them but continue to learn they are no match for the hardiness of the chain. Finally, they give up any further attempts to free themselves.

As adult elephants are conditioned by past experiences, they are now effectively bound by the thinnest of ropes or no rope at all. They do not attempt to wander because they believe they possess no power to break the ties that bind them; therefore, true freedom is no longer available to them. And they relegate themselves to a tamed life within just a small circle, nothing like the powerful creature they were born to be.

Now is the time to break the chains of the myths to unleash personal growth for yourself. You can then, in turn, grow your people and experience exponential business growth.

I'm not going to presume to know exactly what issues you need to work on regarding your personal growth. But, I can share with you five personal growth habits that will help you easily create your own specific personal growth plan— which will clarify what your first item should be on your daily to-do list.

1. Set personal growth objectives.

Plan to learn something new every day and make your growth intentional, strategic, and effective. Become a lifelong learner. Focus on growing in the area where you can add value to your greatest strength, not your weakness. The more you learn, the more you will realize how far you still need to go, and you will gain a hunger to learn more.

If a person will spend one hour a day on the same subject for five years, that person will be an expert on that subject.
—EARL NIGHTINGALE

2. Apply what you learn.

Personal growth is an uphill climb all the way and applying what you learn is the most difficult part. Practice what you learn in ways that help and improve yourself and other people. It will be worth the effort when you realize you know what you've learned so well that you can teach others.

The greatest of all insights is that we cannot be tomorrow what we do not do today.
—JOHN MAXWELL

3. Reflect on what you learn.

Spend time daily reflecting on what you learned. Your reflection on today will motivate you to look forward to tomorrow.

Without reflection, we go blindly on our way, creating more unintended consequences, and failing to achieve anything useful.
—MARGARET J. WHEATLEY

4. Associate with like-minded people.

The people you spend the most time with greatly impact your outlook. If those closest to you are hungry for personal growth and are striving to reach their potential, they will rub off on you. If they have no desire or interest for personal growth, their negative influence will pull you down. Make sure that you're among like-minded people who will encourage and challenge you to reach your full potential.

5. File what you learn.

Start by being on the lookout for anything you hear or read that you want to learn. Then, file it so you can use the information in the future. Begin filing quotes, stories, and ideas that you find as you learn. This habit will yield a great harvest of material for your future use. It will keep you highly focused to go for the good stuff that will stimulate you and help your personal growth.

Take a True North Bearing

Has your personal growth been bound by chains? What are you doing to unleash your potential?

Remember, personal growth is a process over time and not a single event. Each day you need to challenge yourself to get a little better and build on the previous day's progress. The same is true for growing your people, as you'll discover in the next chapter.

CHAPTER 5

Grow Your People

Develop Your Team to Live Your Dream

The growth and development of people
is the highest calling of leadership.
—HARVEY S. FIRESTONE

The other day, I ran into a friend from high school. After our initial pleasantries and greetings, my friend started to talk about our good ol' high school days.

A few minutes into our chat, I tried to turn the conversation to what was going on in his life now. But, he repeatedly turned the focus back to what happened in high school and was uninterested in talking about the present or the future.

As we discussed in the last chapter, once we graduate from high school or college, we tend to lose much of the discipline we developed to study for a test, read a book, or write a paper. Therefore, we must become more intentional if we want to continue learning and growing after we leave the structure of formal education.

What's true for us as leaders is also true for our people. Just as it is crucial for us to lift the lid off our personal growth, it is also important that we guide and facilitate the growth of our people.

People, in general, are preoccupied with the busyness of life and often satisfied with the memories of the past (like my high school buddy). When they get stuck in the rut of the status quo, it limits their expectations of change and a better future.

Their thinking can become too small or narrow in scope. They often see only one solution, or no solution, to grow their career or business or to make quality improvements. They have limited their exposure to new ideas by associating with the same people, doing the same thing, and repeating the same experiences, over and over. They don't see themselves in a larger way, beyond where they are now, reaching for the next level.

> *While we don't always get what we want, we always get what we choose.*
> —JOHN MAXWELL

Because many people will not grow on their own, you must intentionally *grow your people*, or you will experience a lid on your business growth. In contrast, if you are willing to invest in and grow your people, you will experience significant results. But, it will require discipline—both in you and in your organization.

> *Discipline is doing what you don't want to do today so you can do what you want to do tomorrow.*

Your employees need to see you, as the leader, actively investing in personal growth, not only for yourself but for them as well. They need a leader who will intentionally grow and stretch them. Think about it: if you do not invest in yourself, who will? Well . . . if you don't invest in your people's growth, who will?

As the years have gone by, I have found many of my high school and college friends stopped advancing in life and work. They have found themselves doing the same thing, with the same people, with the same life and work for all these years. Once they finished high school or college, they were "finished" with personal growth, and, therefore, they put a lid on their life and work. They lacked the discipline to pursue personal growth.

As the leader of your organization, you must not settle for stagnation for you or your people. So, let's get started.

Take a True North Bearing

Do you want to grow your business? What are you doing to invest in your employees' personal growth?

Training *or* Development?

According to Culture Amp, a platform for compiling employee feedback, one of the top-three drivers for employee engagement in 2018 is "learning and development."[9] Devoting time and resources to grow your people will improve the engagement of your people, which will positively impact your entire organization.

I learned this firsthand not long after I became the leader of our family company. Once I began regularly working ON as well as IN the business, I began to see a bit of daylight and some opportunities to increase revenue. As I mentioned earlier, by the end of 1974, something amazing happened. With a whole lot of people helping me, we more than tripled our revenue, and we generated the highest profit in the history of the business.

Foreseeing that revenue increase, I had to also triple the number of employees for our summer peak season. So, I hired mostly students (looking for a full-time summer job) from the local university.

---

9   Josh Sloan, "Insights from Culture Amp's 2018 Employee Benchmarks," Culture Amp blog, https://blog.cultureamp.com/2018-employee-benchmarks, accessed May 11, 2018.

I quickly joined one of my industry's (moving and storage) trade associations, which had some excellent packing skills training material that I could use to train our current and new employees. This was one way I could help them become the best employees possible.

I will never forget the phrase used in that training material, which was repeated over and over: "How you *act* is as important as how you *pack*." Wow, how true that statement is, even today!

"How you act" is your personal development or people skills.

"How you pack" is about your technical training or job skills.

To be honest with you, in the early years, I did not know there was even a difference between training and development, even though I was doing both. Since then, I have observed that the words *training* and *development* are mostly used together in the business world. However, there is a very distinct difference between them, one often overlooked by most leaders. What is the difference between training and development? Please see the following chart.

	Training	Development
Focus	What you do; your current job or role	Who you are becoming as a person
Purpose	Improve performance with knowledge and/or skills	Prepare for future potential and overall growth
Directed toward	Organization's needs	Person's needs
Horizon	Short-term (present)	Long-term (future)
Mode	Immediate need (an event)	Career (a process)
Desired Outcome	Efficiency	Effectiveness
Emphasis	Specific job or role requirement; tangible	Conceptual and general knowledge; intangible
Prepares for	Increased productivity	Future capability
Goals	Specific and well defined; measurable	Open-ended and ongoing; challenging to evaluate
Responsibility	The organization	The individual (initiated by the organization)
Led by	Trainer	The individual (initiated by the organization)
Intention	Drive for results	Enhance relationships
Focal point	Managing things	Leading people
Concerned about	What we say and do	How we say and do it

Training *and* Development

As the years went by and our business kept growing, I added all types of job-related knowledge and skills training during the nonpeak seasons. But, I also began to understand that I needed to develop people as well so that each person could reach his or her full potential.

Just as Jim Collins's principle of the genius of the AND applies to relationships *and* results, it also validates our pursuit of both training *and* development.

Once training has occurred, the organization will expect its employees to practice their newly acquired skills and master them, causing greater revenue, reduced expenses, and increased productivity, thereby adding value to the organization and its customers.

And once development has occurred in the leader and his employees, they are all considered to be value-added assets to the organization and its customers. Enhancing emotional maturity, along with achieving a greater professional edge, is what development is all about.

You can see it is not either/or but both training *and* development.

Every leader can spark business growth by creating a workplace culture that embraces both training and *development.*

Take a True North Bearing

Are you ready to work ON, not just IN, the business? How do you plan to apply training and development in your business?

What Is Your Bent?

As our business kept growing, I had less and less time to help around the house. I'm so thankful that my wife agreed to become the plumber, the electrician, and the person to take care of the yard, a whole host of trees, and the swimming pool. She paid all our personal bills along with chauffeuring our three boys and their friends.

I could not have done all that I accomplished without her. You know what is amazing? She really likes doing all that stuff. Lucky me! In fact, you can just imagine what her favorite cable channel is. It's HGTV, especially the show *Fixer Upper*. She loves learning new, practical, step-by-step home refurbishing skills. She loves the training, the how-to. It's her bent.

As for me, I have spent years attending training for new moving and storage industry skills and even non-industry-specific skills. However, my bent has always been in developing people.

In doing so, I live out one of my core values, "achieve significance," and fulfill my purpose, which is to "make a difference in people, for people, and through people." My values statement is simply, "people, people, people." When I accomplish all this, it gives me energy; I get excited, and passion swells up in me.

I do everything in my ability to never fall short in developing people. It is my bent, my strength.

Take a True North Bearing

Where is your bent, your strength? How do you feel when you live contrary to your natural bent?

Despite the wonderful advice in that packing training material I found long ago, I have discovered that most leaders in the moving and storage industry, and in other industries as well, are interested *only* in training their people.

The development of people is undervalued. Leaders seem to expect people to just know how to behave on the job. They tend to assume everyone knows and understands the importance of being on time, taking initiative, being friendly, and producing high-quality work.

To get and keep a job, people usually need a full list of technical and knowledge skills that were acquired through training. Doctors must go through years of training to become a medical doctor. Dentists need to know how to fill your cavities. Accountants need to be certified. Plumbers and electricians spend a great deal of time as an apprentice. Manufacturing workers need several hours of training to operate equipment or machinery safely and efficiently. Personal assistants need to accurately type eighty-plus words per minute. Even workers who perform moving services need packing, loading, and unloading skills training. The list could go on and on.

Yet, most customers and even employers make decisions based on factors beyond the technical skills someone possesses to do the job.

- Which medical doctor do you go to? The one who is kind and friendly and takes time to be with you or the one who sees you as only a body count to bill for?
- Which dentist do you go to? The one who is pleasant and fun to be around and takes time to answer your questions or the one who treats you like a number in a long line of mouths and molars?
- Which accountant do you go to? One who has a strong work ethic and is a great encourager to his coworkers or one who hits the door at five o'clock, regardless of peak demand time, and doesn't appreciate those who work for him?
- Which service worker do you retain when times are lean? The one with a positive attitude, open and willing to help, or the one who is inflexible and not willing to admit mistakes?

Regardless of the position or job mentioned above, personal development is the true difference maker between workers with equal skill levels. Training is not enough—and neither is development.

Your training in technical job skills may get your foot in the door. However, your personal development/ people skills will keep opening future doors that are crucial to your career and business success.

Because of this, as the years went by, I learned to hire people who complemented me and who were better than I was at driving for results and managing the business because I knew my strength was enhancing relationships and leading my employees. Not surprisingly, our leadership team was better at the technical job skills training than I was. I also began to understand that I was stronger at developing our people, which I really enjoyed doing.

Focus on improving the person, not just the work he gets done.
—John Maxwell

Whether you have a bent toward learning and training technical job skills or a bent toward personal development and people skills, one thing is for sure: every organization needs training *and* development.

Take a True North Bearing

Are you more comfortable with training or development? Do you have a plan for training? Do you have a plan for development? Is there someone in your Human Resource department with whom you could share this plan?

Remember the Effectiveness Quotient from part 1? As our company kept growing over the years, I observed that the returns on investment in training and development to grow myself and to grow our people gave us extraordinary business growth. Why? Because when you invest in relationships *and* results, your effectiveness is multiplied.

So, as you work ON your business, in addition to setting aside time to grow yourself, you'll want to focus on growing your people through training and development. Even if it requires extra effort and time, even if it takes you out of your comfort zone, the exponentially larger results will speak for themselves.

How to Grow Your People

Here are some specific strategies I used to stimulate the personal growth of our people that can apply to any industry and all company sizes.

1. We regularly and carefully selected industry and non-industry leadership, personal development, and skill improvement seminars, education sessions, and video training for our people to attend. We planned our major personal growth events and training during our annually reoccurring slow season. We also scheduled our training on nonpeak days and during typically slower business hours.

2. I felt so strongly about growing our people that we would have half-day, company-wide workshops every year. These workshops created opportunities for us to learn and grow together as a team, like when we introduced the ON/IN leadership practice, as you'll see in the next chapter.

3. I also led our people and our leadership team in book discussions. Typically, we would review one chapter per month. Some of the best and most impactful book reviews we ever did were *The 21 Irrefutable Laws of Leadership* by John Maxwell and *Built to Last* and *Good to Great* by Jim Collins. I would recommend you do the same with my book *Principled Profits: Outward Success Is an Inside Job* and this book.

4. Some of our people even listened to personal development and leadership podcasts while they drove to and from work or while they exercised.

Take a True North Bearing

What strategies and plans could you begin implementing to start growing your people? How could you leverage your slower periods of the month or year to increase the effectiveness of your people through training and development?

Once you have committed to grow yourself first and then grow your people, you will be able to grow your business, as you'll see in the next chapter.

CHAPTER 6

Grow Your Business

Collaborate to Accelerate Growth

None of us is as smart as all of us.
—KEN BLANCHARD

The other day, I ate breakfast at Chick-fil-A. The food was delicious, and their uncommon and consistent customer service was excellent as usual. If you have been to Chick-fil-A, then you have had the same experience, which exceeds expectations. In my company, we called this a Triple-E experience.

Did you know that Chick-fil-A generates more revenue per restaurant than any other fast-food chain, and they are only open six days a week? Why are they so successful? Why are they dominating fast food in an industry notorious for poor service and high turnover?

They have chosen a growth strategy, which is to invest in their employees with training and development. In doing so, the employees know, "You care for me! You treat me like a real person." Chick-fil-A has learned a key principle in business: "to serve, not to be served."

Training and development must start with you as the leader (because you cannot teach what you do not know) and then with your people. Before you can grow your business, you must first serve your people with training and development, just like Chick-fil-A does. Then you can lead.

Personal Growth for You and Your People Leads to Business Growth

Since training is quick and straightforward, communicating how to do a job, most people learn the mechanics of their work very rapidly. Thus, training usually occurs in hours, days, or even months, but development always take more time. You cannot rush development because it is a process. In contrast, training is usually an event—something you can do once and then you are done.

The following are seven personal growth benefits of training and development for you, as the leader, and your people.

1. You will become a better person.

Employees will feel that you care for them, that you are interested in them as people and want to help them become better people, better moms, dads, friends, or servants in the community.

2. You will maximize your potential.

When you are investing in your personal growth and creating training and development opportunities, your employees will feel the effects and say, "You foster a learning environment so I can do the best job I know how."

They sense that you see training and development as an investment and not an expense. Employees will avoid personal and professional stagnation: doing the same thing, at the same place, with the same people, hoping the same hopes, and never winning new victories. Instead, they will truly want to achieve and receive recognition for their achievements.

Leaders who consider others' needs first are more likely to empower employees.
—MATT TENNEY

3. You can anticipate explosive growth.

Personal growth is not an automatic process. Nor is business growth. As you raise your effectiveness today, the greater the chance you will be more effective tomorrow.

> *In order to do more, I've got to be more.*
> —JIM ROHN

4. You will enjoy change.

Once people are willing to change on the inside, they will not only accept organizational and market condition changes but seek them. For without change, there can be no growth.

5. You will attract high achievers.

When you develop a reputation of valuing personal growth in your organization, you will attract more high achievers. Why? High achievers want to make a difference because they believe they have much to give.

6. You will experience teamwork.

Customers and suppliers (yes, even suppliers) will feel the impact of teamwork—excellence in communication, coordination, and cooperation among the team. Why? Team players want and are motivated "to serve, not to be served."

> *Teamwork makes the dream work.*
> —JOHN MAXWELL

7. You will grow the business.

Employees will come to work each day with excitement, enthusiasm, and passion because you, as the leader, have earned these things.

Now, you are ready to grow your business. Now, you are ready to set your business apart from the crowded marketplace and work ON, not just IN, the business.

By the way, the next time you are in the Chick-fil-A drive-thru and say, "Thank you," the employee will always reply, "My pleasure."

The "my pleasure" policy instituted by the company founder, Truett Cathy, was inspired by a visit to the Ritz Carlton. When Cathy said, "Thank you," to the man behind the counter, he responded, "My pleasure."

Out of this exchange, Chick-fil-A's novel idea was born: treat customers as if they're at a luxury establishment. This model continues to distinguish Chick-fil-A from its competitors, highlighting the importance of the little ways you communicate with customers.

Take a True North Bearing

Have you found it difficult to lead your employees toward delivering world-class results? Are you open to serve first, then lead second?

Every Employee Asks These Five Questions

For my first Olympic-distance triathlon, I trained with a good friend twice a day, six days a week. We scheduled our training around each other's personal and work schedules. During our weekly training, we found that our strengths complemented each other very well:

- I was the morning person who would give him a wake-up call to meet for our training before going to work.
- We had about the same pace when swimming in a pool.
- He was a stronger runner than me, so he paced me well.
- I was stronger on the bicycle, so I would pace him well.

- We enjoyed each other's company, so it made all the hard training go by quickly. It didn't even seem like we were training hard.

While a training partner helped me immensely as I prepared for triathlons, for many years, I was doing my company's business planning alone and in a vacuum. Not good.

Eventually, as I continued to practice the ON/IN concept, I came to understand the importance and value of getting our employees to partner with me in the planning and decision-making process. This collaborative approach became key in growing our business.

If leaders don't take time to proactively plan and include their people in the planning and decision-making process, their employees will become dissatisfied and frustrated. Employees need to feel involved, understood, and appreciated. The better the employees are, the more they expect to know what is going on. And the more they deserve to know, the more frustrated they are when they don't know.

Every employee wants answers to the following five questions from their leaders:

1. Where is the company headed?
2. What is my role in this effort?
3. How is my performance going to be evaluated?
4. How have I been doing?
5. How could I do better?

Employees want more than just being told, told, told. They want to be asked to think. They want to be involved in the decision-making process. They want access to their supervisors, input in the setting of objectives, and recognition for their achievements.

As the leader, how well do you interact with your employees? How about asking yourself the following three questions:

1. How am I doing as a leader?

2. How could I be more effective as a leader?

3. How would I like to have myself as a supervisor?

Take a True North Bearing

How did you, as the leader, answer the five employee questions listed above? Do your employees work well as a team? How would you like to work for you?

Our First ON/IN Workshop

In the fall of 1999, I wanted to get our employees involved in our proactive planning process as our normal way of doing business. That is when I introduced the ON/IN technique during a company-wide half-day workshop.

Since our company had several different business functions and business units, I worked very hard with each leader of each function and unit to prepare for the meeting. The leaders developed a PowerPoint presentation to explain their answers to the following three questions:

1. Where have we been?

2. Where are we now?

3. Where are we going?

Each leader made his presentation to the entire company assembled at the meeting.

After the leaders finished their presentations, we asked employees from each function and business unit to sit as a group. Within each group, we sat no more than eight people at a table to encourage interaction and discussion. Next, the table groups used flip charts to record their ideas and answers to the three follow-up questions related to question three above, "Where are we going?":

1. How can we get there?
2. When do we want to arrive?
3. Who can make it happen on schedule?

One month following the first ON/IN workshop, we held a second company-wide half-day workshop on the ON/IN practice. Each leader of a function or business unit reported back to the whole company using a slide presentation that displayed the results and progress they had made based on their table discussions in the first meeting.

Again, we got every employee from each function or business unit to sit as a group, with no more than eight people at a table. Then, they used flip charts to facilitate and record their observations and answers to the following two questions:

1. What do our customers want to buy from us?
2. How can/do we give them what they want?

Then, each table reported back to the entire company what they discussed.

As we wrapped up our second workshop, I had each table address one more company-specific question since we would be moving soon to a new location: what barriers or challenges will there be for us at the new location? The depth of the results from all the discussions to this final question was amazing. We captured excellent ideas from the reports we heard from each table.

Remember the participative process of goals and controls from part 1? The key is to

1. Ask and then listen.
2. Involve your entire team in a collaborative effort to find the answers so that you and your people will grow from being involved in the participative decision-making process.

We learned that the more our people participated in the decision-making process, the better they understood where we were going, and they grew by their involvement in the process.

Take a True North Bearing

Have you ever struggled to grow your business? Would you consider involving your entire team in the process above?

ON/IN: The Eighth Wonder of the World?

Every day for two to three hours, I read numerous articles and books, watch videos and news programs, and listen to podcasts and many other sources for my personal growth. On one recent day, I came across what was said to be a true story by Joy Garrison Wasson, an English teacher in Muncie, Indiana. She taught English for thirty years, and she died in 2005 at the age of only sixty-two:

> *A group of students was asked to list what they thought were the present Seven Wonders of the World. Though there were some disagreements, the following received the most votes:*
>
> 1. *Egypt's Great Pyramids*
> 2. *Taj Mahal*
> 3. *Grand Canyon*
> 4. *Panama Canal*
> 5. *Empire State Building*
> 6. *St. Peter's Basilica*
> 7. *China's Great Wall*

While gathering the votes, the teacher noted that one student had not finished her paper yet. So, she asked the girl if she was having trouble with her list. The girl replied, "Yes, a little. I couldn't quite make up my mind because there are so many."

The teacher said, "Well, tell us what you have, and maybe we can help."

The girl hesitated, then read, "I think the Seven Wonders of the World are

1. *To see*
2. *To hear*
3. *To touch*
4. *To taste*
5. *To feel*
6. *To laugh*
7. *And to love."*

The room was so quiet you could have heard a pin drop. The things we overlook as simple and ordinary and that we take for granted are truly wondrous![10]

I remember well when I overlooked the simple and ordinary, and I took for granted the truly "wondrous" opportunity to work ON, not just IN, my business.

Working ON, not just IN, the business means taking time to ask, "What work *should* I be doing?" It means focusing your time and energy not just on doing your work but also on how your work could be done more effectively and efficiently. It means making intentional, proactive plans to improve revenues, control costs, increase productivity, and enhance the nature and extent of the value rendered to your customers. It employs the three-part strategy:

10 "The Other Seven Wonders," Wisdom Stories to Live By (blog), August 3, 2012, https://philipchircop.wordpress.com/tag/teacher/ .

1. Grow yourself.
2. Grow your people.
3. Grow your business.

Take a True North Bearing

What is one thing you could implement now to help grow your business?

_____

Now that you have your roadmap for your True North Business journey, it's time to find your WOW!

PART THREE

WOW!

CHAPTER 7

Why Do We
Stop Asking Why?

---

*Curiosity May Have Killed the Cat,
but It's the Key to Growth*

*One of life's fundamental truths states, "Ask and you shall receive."
As kids we get used to asking for things, but somehow we lose this
ability in adulthood. We come up with all sorts of excuses and
reasons to avoid any possibility of criticism or rejection.*
—JACK CANFIELD

One day I observed one of my grandsons interact with his mom. She had just made a comment about something, and it sparked his curiosity. His first response was to place his little palms on each side of her face and turn her face toward his determined gaze. Then he said in a very innocent way (and, of course, sweetly, like all grandchildren), "*Why*, Mommy, *why?*"

I remember all three of our boys, when they were young, would also often ask the why question. And I'm sure you have experienced this in your own children or observed it in other children. In fact, sometimes their insistent why questions seem a bit like the drip, drip, drip of water torture. But . . .

*Everyone can learn more by adopting and encouraging
the childlike practice of asking why.*

Why do children use such a profound question and with such innocence? Between ages two and three, children develop the cognitive ability to make logical connections, and this advance sparks the following behavior:

- Curiosity and eagerness to explore this fascinating world
- Desire to explore with the people they feel the safest around and love the most
- Drive to learn and understand why things happen
- Push to ask why, which reflects a thirst for knowledge
- Use of new critical skills that help them gain a much more complex understanding of how the world works, via what they see, hear, and do
- Understanding that the more they ask why the more they learn

Children start off endlessly asking questions, but then gradually ask fewer and fewer questions as they progress through grade school.

A *Newsweek* story, "The Creativity Crisis," described the signs of declining creativity among our school children. The article cited an interesting fact that preschool kids ask their parents an average of one hundred questions a day. Wow! However, by middle school, they've basically stopped asking questions. It is also around this time that student motivation and engagement drop like a rock.[11]

If kids get so many benefits from asking why, why do they eventually stop? It was found that our educational system rewarded students for having the answer, not for asking good questions. We have an answers-driven school system.

*Knowing the answers to questions will help you in school.
Knowing how to ask questions will help you in life.*
—WARREN BERGER

---

11 Po Bronson and Ashley Merryman, "The Creativity Crisis," *Newsweek* (online), July 10, 2010, https://www.newsweek.com/creativity-crisis-74665.

It's sad that as adults we carry this answer-driven mentality into our personal and work life, and we don't do very well at asking the powerful, one-word question: why?

Why > What and How

In our modern society, people always tend to ask what and how first. They feel those types of questions are more important than any other.

However, those who really make a difference ask why first and then go on to figure out the best what and how. The why enables you to find the best whats and hows because the why is your passion applied toward what you are doing.

And we often neglect the importance of asking why in the workplace. In most organizations, the bosses manage, and employees do what they're told. However, that thinking is counterproductive because we, as leaders, have employees who don't know *why* they're doing what they are doing. And the why provides the motivation.

Plus, we have people on the front line who often bring better ideas forward because they challenge traditional practices. Innovation and creativity are not the exclusive domain of leadership. We should pay attention to those employees who respectfully ask why because they are demonstrating an interest in their jobs and exhibiting a curiosity that could position them as future leaders within your organization.

So, as adults and as leaders, let's learn from children and ask perhaps the most important question: why?

Take a True North Bearing

Have you stopped asking the question why? As a leader, how are you encouraging your employees to ask why?

Ask Why Now, Reap Six Benefits Later

I was a curious young boy, and I truly enjoyed exploring. And I loved to get on my little bicycle (especially early on Saturday mornings) and ride slowly through our neighborhood, just looking all around. I went farther than my parents ever knew because I was fascinated with the world I was seeing, and I had a thirst to learn.

I started asking why as a very young boy, and I have never stopped. Having the childlike quality of asking why will help you learn something new every day.

I don't just want knowledge; I want understanding.
—BOBBY ALBERT

Every person should ask why because of the following six benefits.

1. You will understand who you are.

As you go through your day, with your antenna up, continually observe and ask yourself the following questions:

- Why did I say what I just said?
- Why was it important for me to say it that way?
- Why did I do what I just did?
- Why was it important for me to do it that way?

The power of these why questions will make you more aware of your actions and teach you more about yourself—your motives and purposes in life.

2. You will know where you are going.

Do you know where you are headed? Why or why not? Are you comfortable being on autopilot, doing the same thing with the same people and talking about the same things?

If you do what you've always done, you'll get what you've always gotten.
—TONY ROBBINS

Are you doing what you love doing? Have you asked why? Are you where you want to be in life? Have you asked why? Your answer to your why question may just take you in a new direction.

3. You will achieve new levels of significance.

I don't know about you, but I want to make a difference.

I want to make a difference in people, for people, and through people.
—BOBBY ALBERT

When you want to make a difference, change occurs in people and in this world. When you ask why, you are asking because it matters, and the answer will shape what you do next.

Many times, asking why will lead to new ways you can help others. Also, asking why about important topics will highlight them, bring awareness, and instigate change. That is making a difference!

4. You will face your fears.

Do you regularly avoid asking yourself the why question out of faith or fear? Do you have an unhealthy habit, behavior, or relationship? Why do you continue? Do you avoid the why question at all costs because you already know the answer or you feel guilty? Does fear stop you from asking that vital question? Does this reluctance hinder you rather than help you develop relationships?

When you ask why, you're looking at your life under a microscope, which will help you deal with whatever fear or pain you hold deep within. As you face your fears and thoughtfully ask why, you can evaluate your life with honesty and respect. This positions you to take your next step in faith instead of fear.

5. You will enhance your relationships.

When you show genuine interest in another person, you make her feel important and worthy. And one of the best ways to encourage a good intellectual conversation and lift up the other person is to ask the question why. Doing this stimulates enthusiasm and motivation in the other person. Most of all, you learn a lot more about her.

Asking questions and listening does more to enhance relationships than we think. Almost always, the person answering the questions comes away feeling you are a wonderful person to know, even though all you did was ask questions and listen.

6. You will add value to others.

When you openly and respectfully challenge yourself with the why question, it will inspire others to do the same. When others see that you are growing and progressing through life because of your curiosity and fearlessness, they will want to have the same kind of life. It will encourage and inspire others to get what they want out of life, too.

Well, it's time to get on your bicycle and explore your neighborhood of life. You can start by asking the most important question: why.

Take a True North Bearing

Are you ready to continually ask the question why? Which of the six benefits listed above will you claim today by intentionally asking why?

Is Your Why Big Enough to Succeed?

According to the Small Business Administration, approximately two-thirds of businesses survive at least two years, about half survive at least five years, and only a third survive at least ten years.[12]

Do you want your organization not just to survive but thrive into the next decade? All leaders can help their business stay the course by overcoming one challenge: embracing a why that is large enough to carry their organization forward. Founders, owners, and leaders must ask themselves

- Is my why bigger than me?
- Is my why bigger than my current business or current job responsibilities?

When I found my why, I found my way.
When I found my why, I found my will.
When I found my why, I found my wings.
—JOHN MAXWELL

Take a True North Bearing

How strong is your why? Is your why bigger than you?

Asking why is not just an academic question; it has bottom-line results. In a study done at the University of Pennsylvania's Wharton School of Business, researchers divided employees at the university call center, where they solicited

---

12 "Table 7: Survival of Private Sector Establishments by Opening Year" (from March 2007 to March 2017), Business Employment Dynamics, Bureau of Labor Statistics, United States Department of Labor, https://www.bls.gov/bdm/us_age_naics_00_table7.txt, accessed March 13, 2018.

donations from alumni, into three groups, each of which was prepped for making calls in a different way:

- Group one interacted in person with beneficiaries of the donations.
- Group two read stories from beneficiaries about how the donations helped them with their education, careers, and lives.
- Group three had no contact at all with the beneficiaries.

After a month of calling, researchers found that group one raised significantly more money than the other groups.[13]

Group one's deeper understanding of the impact of their work on students who benefitted from the money raised—the why—motivated them to get better results. What you do and how you do it are important, but the why gives the passion (the fuel, the energy) to succeed.

The person who knows "how" will always have a job.
The person who knows "why" will always be his boss.
—DIANE RAVITCH

When leaders find their why deep within, only then will they have the passion and professional will to resolve to do whatever it takes to make the company great, no matter how big or hard the decision.

How do you know if your why is strong enough? Ask yourself these questions:

- Is passion a characteristic of your life?
- Do you wake up feeling enthusiastic about your day?

---

13   Adam M. Grant, Elizabeth Campbell, Grace Chen, David Lapedis, and Keenan Cottone, "Impact and the Art of Motivation Maintenance: The Effects of Contact with Beneficiaries on Persistence Behavior," *Organizational Behavior and Human Decision Processes*, vol. 103, no. 1 (May 2007), pp. 53–67, https://doi.org/10.1016/j.obhdp.2006.05.004. "Putting a Face to a Name: The Art of Motivating Employees," Knowledge@Wharton (website), February 17, 2010, http://knowledge.wharton.upenn.edu/article/putting-a-face-to-a-name-the-art-of-motivating-employees/.

- Is the first day of the week your favorite, or do you live from weekend to weekend, sleepwalking through your everyday routine?
- How long has it been since you couldn't sleep because you were too excited by an idea?

Does your passion show? To get an honest assessment, just ask your coworkers. Ask your spouse about your level of desire.

Business failure rates have much to do with leaders not honestly asking the why question of themselves. Instead, these leaders assume the leadership role without the passion and professional will their organization needs to succeed for the decades to come.

Think about it. If you, as the leader, lack passion and professional will, how do you think your employees are going to behave after watching you?

Take a True North Bearing

If you left your business today, would your stakeholders understand their why well enough to continue on?

For a why strong enough to succeed, I have found that leaders need to take the time to discover both their personal life purpose and their organization's purpose. Why? Because as a leader, your life purpose also affects the lives of the people around you.

If your why doesn't seem strong enough for your life or your business, then it's time to find one that is. It's time for you to discover why you exist—your "one thing"—your life purpose. Not just because your business needs it but because *you* need it. So, let's lead ourselves first and begin with discovering our life purpose.

CHAPTER 8

Discover Your Life Purpose

What Were You Born to Do?

A man's true delight is to do the things he was made for.
—MARCUS AURELIUS

My natural tendency is to be in a hurry. In fact, the word *rush* accurately characterized my daily routine for many years. I rushed to get out of bed: like a fireman, when my alarm went off, I was already going down the pole. I rushed to exercise: I usually exercise six mornings per week. I rushed to clean up. I rushed to get to work. I rushed from one business appointment to the next appointment, from one phone call to the next. I rushed to a meeting after hours or to one of our boys' soccer games. Next, I rushed to dinner. Then, finally, I rushed back to get in bed so I could start the cycle all over at four thirty the next morning.

I'm tired even just writing about all of this frenetic rushing around. It sounds like a gerbil spinning in his cage. But, weren't all these things good to do?

Nature does not hurry, yet everything is accomplished.
—LAO TZU

Why do you do what you do each day? Why do you get out of bed? Do you get up and do what's necessary to simply receive a paycheck? Or, is there something bigger happening?

Are you too busy building a career or a business and trying to become financially secure? Is your work the center of your identity and life? Are you rushing around without a life purpose?

Are you forever talking about the Promised Land, but you can't bring yourself to leave your familiar territory—a known place that feels like home, even if not a great one? Do you hear that still, small voice telling you to move on to something better, but you regularly push it aside? You know that voice is true, but you also know that to follow it would lead you into unfamiliar, uncharted territory.

Do you keep telling yourself any of these lines?

- "It would be better to wait until I'm finished with what I'm doing."
- "I'm too tired."
- "I'll do it someday" (knowing that "someday" never seems to come).

I discovered that my calendar was filled with activity but not necessarily accomplishment. Finding my life purpose helped me prioritize where to apply my time, talent, and treasures.

Once you understand your life purpose, you will prioritize your life according to that purpose. Without a clear life purpose, you'll get off track, and you may never feel a real sense of fulfillment and completion.

A person with a clear purpose will make progress on even the roughest road. A person with no purpose will make no progress on even the smoothest road.
—THOMAS CARLYLE

Take a True North Bearing

Do you know why you exist? Are you rushing around without a life purpose? Will you take time to pause, reflect, and evaluate your life?

Two Key Benefits

If your why doesn't seem strong enough for your life or your business, then it's time to find one that is. Every person should discover their life purpose because of two key benefits.

1. Passion

The first benefit of knowing your life purpose is passion. Why is passion so important? You can either surrender to your circumstances, or you can surrender to a cause that is so great, your circumstances won't matter.

When you surrender to your circumstances, you will have good days and bad days. You are at the mercy of what happens *to* you. But, when you surrender to a cause or purpose, you have good days wherever you go. The purpose never dies. Your passion will help you conclude that it didn't matter what happened to you so long as the purpose continues because it is all about what has happened *in* you.

Passion is the fuel for the will. When you discover what you want and want it badly enough, you can find the willpower to achieve it. And, you are a more dedicated and productive person.

A leader with great passion and few skills always outperforms a leader with great skills and no passion.
—JOHN MAXWELL

Passion also gives you energy and credibility. When you love what you do and do what you love, others find it inspiring. Do you know anyone who became successful at something they hate?

> *Success is waking up in the morning, whoever you are, wherever you are, however old or young, and bounding out of bed because there's something out there that you love to do, that you believe in, that you're good at—something that's bigger than you are, and you can hardly wait to get at it again today.*
> —WHIT HOBBS

That's what passion does for a leader. Passion in a leader is compelling to others, and people want to follow passionate leaders.

2. Progress

The second benefit of knowing your life purpose is progress. Purpose gives you drive. It shows you a destination. It paints a picture of your future. It energizes you. And it makes obstacles and problems seem small in comparison to its importance.

Without a clear life purpose, you'll continually get off track, and you may never feel a real sense of fulfillment and completion. Once you understand your life purpose, you will prioritize your life according to that purpose.

> *If you have a purpose in which you can believe, there's no end to the amount of things you can accomplish.*
> —MARIAN ANDERSON

Time to Pause, Reflect, and Evaluate

You may be wondering, "Bobby, what did you discover to be your life purpose?" First, I want you to know that my journey to understand why I exist was a multistep process. It all started when I read the book *In Search of Excellence* by Tom Peters and

Robert Waterman. This led me to prepare a company mission statement for my business. The process of identifying our company mission statement motivated me to begin to pause, reflect, and think more about my personal mission and purpose in life. Then I read the book *Choose Your Attitudes, Change Your Life* by Robert Jeffress. While reading this book, I discovered my life purpose.

The reason why I exist is to be a model Christian businessman. Knowing my life purpose is like knowing true north in every area of my life, not just at work. It serves to properly orient me, even if my circumstances and surroundings change. It set me on the course from success to significance.

Since then, I've developed a process to help leaders discover their personal why. It doesn't matter whether you start with your organization, like I did, or with yourself; what's important is that you don't give up until you find your purpose—and then help your organization find its purpose.

Do you also have a burning desire to move from success to significance, to discover something more meaningful that rises above perks and paychecks at work? Understanding why you exist can fulfill this desire in your own life and give you a deep sense of meaning and purpose.

Your life purpose is the reason why you were uniquely made and placed on this planet. When you discover it, it is like a beacon that shows the way in every area of your life.

As a leader, you are accustomed to listening to consultants, supervisors, employees, and market research. Now it's time to listen to your inner voice. It is time to take stock, listen, and learn. Stop rushing around. Pause, reflect, and evaluate your life so that you are ready to listen to that interior voice and discover why you exist, your life purpose.

Take a True North Bearing

Do you know why you exist? Are you rushing around without a life purpose? Will you take time to pause, reflect, and evaluate?

What Is Your Life Purpose?

Here is an exercise you can use to discover your own life purpose.

1. What do you care deeply about?

This question is about your passion, about discovering that thing that really excites you. To answer this question, ask yourself

- What is my deepest passion?
- How am I wired?
- What makes me tick?
- If I could meet any need in the world, what need would I meet?
- If I do not meet this need, who will?

2. What have you achieved?

This question is about your competence, about discovering that special something you're good at. When your skills are sharp and when you home in on the one thing that is your strength, it will make you say, "I was born to do this." To answer this question, ask yourself

- What have I done uncommonly well?
- What do I do so well that I would enjoy doing it without pay? What do I find so fulfilling about it?
- What do I want to be doing for the next ten or twenty years?
- What gifts have been given to me that I want to use?
- What abilities do I have that others tend to notice and affirm?
- If I could give a how-to seminar to a group, what topic would I choose?
- What single word best describes the area in which I am both interested and gifted?

The more questions you can answer, the greater the number of clues you'll have to help you reveal your why.

If a man is called to be a street sweeper, he should sweep streets even as Michelangelo painted or Beethoven composed music or Shakespeare wrote poetry. He should sweep streets so well that all the hosts of heaven and earth will pause to say, "Here lived a great street sweeper who did his job well."
—Martin Luther King Jr.

3. Where do your passion and competence intersect?

As you look deep inside, the combination of your highest passion and your highest competency is what I consider to be your life purpose—the answer to the question, "Why do I exist?"

To answer this question, look back at your answers to the two previous questions in this section. What one or two words continually surface for you?

Allow these words to help you complete the following important sentence: the reason why I exist is _____. This sentence is your life purpose statement. It's your why. Remember, the more concise your life purpose statement is, the better.

Discovering your life purpose is a process. It will take time to learn about yourself, but the process is as important as the product. The key is to be authentic and be yourself. There is only one of you to do what you were created for. When you identify your true life purpose, you will know.

If you'd like to download my Life Purpose Discovery Worksheet so you have these questions printed out for you, you can do that at TNB-book.com.

Take a True North Bearing

Have you allowed yourself the time to discover your life purpose—or have you scheduled time to do it in the near future? Will you be authentic to yourself?

Living Your Life Purpose

Once I discovered why I exist (my life purpose), the first question I asked myself was, "Now what?" That is when I realized I needed to start living my life purpose. So, the next logical question was, "How do I live out my life purpose?"

Every successful life purpose needs some structure, an agenda to act upon, because you now understand that . . .

> *Your life purpose is not something you want to do, but something you have to do. It is why you exist.*

The following three steps will help you create an agenda to act upon:

1. Share

Initiate conversations and share your life purpose with your spouse and other people you trust and respect, such as family members, close friends, and coworkers. Share the journey you went through to discover why you exist. Then, ask them a few follow-up questions:

- What do you think about it?
- What questions do you have?
- Do you have suggestions about how I could live out my life purpose?
- Will you help keep me honest and true to my life purpose?

Use this important step of sharing to create accountability and recruit their support.

As for me, I found that when I began to share my life purpose with others, not only did they confirm it but they also helped me see how I was already living out my life purpose.

2. Write

After sharing and receiving input from others, it is time to write down your answers to the following questions:

- How have you lived out your life purpose in the past—even before you consciously understood your life purpose?
- How are you currently living out your life purpose? (This will give you confidence.)
- How can you live out your life purpose in the future? (Then prioritize your list in order of importance.)

Nothing contributes so much to tranquilize the mind as a steady purpose—a point on which the soul may fix its intellectual eye.
—MARY WOLLSTONECRAFT SHELLEY

3. Act

This is like putting legs under your life purpose and taking action on how to live it out.

First, take your life purpose and internalize it; it needs to become a part of how you see yourself. I encourage you to print it, post it, and memorize it.

Second, implement one idea on the list you wrote in step two. Choose the one that is the quickest and easiest to accomplish. Evaluate the results and then go to the next priority on your list to express how you are going to live out your life purpose.

Third, begin to integrate your life purpose into your thinking and awareness by committing to the following actions:

- Remember your life purpose when exploring new opportunities.
- Rely on your life purpose when dealing with new challenges.
- Incorporate your life purpose into your decision-making process (For example, you can ask questions like, "How will this decision affect the way I'm living out my life purpose?" and "Which option most closely aligns with and supports my life purpose?").
- Consider your life purpose when planning and managing whatever receives your time and attention—like your personal goals and daily calendar.

What lies behind us and what lies before us are tiny matters compared to what lies within us.
—OLIVER WENDELL HOLMES

Take a True North Bearing

Have you discovered why you exist? How would your life change if you knew your life purpose?

The greatest pleasure and joy of achievement comes from accomplishing what you sense deep inside of you that you *have* to do. Why? It is *why* you exist! And being true to yourself, you will say, "I was born to do this."

CHAPTER 9

Discover Your Organization's Purpose

Empower Your Team with Purpose and Meaning

Singleness of purpose is one of the chief essentials for success in life, no matter what may be one's aim.
—JOHN D. ROCKEFELLER

Are you searching for meaning in your work? Or, more precisely, are you searching for meaningful work? It is impossible to have a great life unless it is a meaningful life.

I have observed that most people are searching for meaningful work—both leaders and employees. Why are so many people searching for meaningful work? Why do people experience such a void and emptiness when they go to work each day? Why are there so many organizations with people drifting along, doing just enough to get by?

There's an old story often told at NASA, in which a janitor was asked what he did for a living. He didn't say, "I'm a janitor." He said, "I'm sending men to the moon!" Wow! He clearly identified with NASA's higher purpose—why they existed—and it empowered him to do his best work.

Would you like to create this kind of meaningful work for yourself and your employees? In this chapter, we'll discuss how to discover your organization's purpose—why you exist. But, to effectively discover and communicate your purpose, there's something else that must come first. It starts with you being a worthy leader your people are willing to follow.

People will follow a worthy leader before they will follow a worthy cause.

So, how do you become a worthy leader? You can only become a worthy leader if you have the trust of your people. Trust is the foundation of worthy leadership. When you have the trust of your people, you can then effectively communicate and model the purpose of your organization. People will forgive occasional mistakes when they know you, as the leader, are bigger on the inside than you are on the outside. But, when you break trust, you forfeit your ability to lead, and you no longer can expect to keep influencing your people.

Leaders earn respect by demonstrating the following four principles:

1. Integrity: Making sound decisions
2. Humility: Admitting your mistakes
3. Authenticity: Being yourself with everyone
4. Selflessness: Putting what's best for your followers and the organization ahead of your personal agenda

Leaders must first believe in their people before their people will believe in them. And leaders must believe in and live out the organization's purpose as well. You can't lead in something you don't believe and practice yourself.

Take a True North Bearing

Have you found meaningful work? Are you the kind of leader
your people truly desire to follow?

The Power of Purpose

Zap! Pow! When I hear those words, I think of the word *power*. I laugh and think about when I was a kid watching the Batman TV series, starring Adam West as Batman and Burt Ward as Robin.

They were known as the "Dynamic Duo," coming to the aid of the Gotham City Police after jumping into their Batmobile. Robin would check the gauges and report, "Atomic batteries to power . . . turbines to speed."

This usually resulted with the two crime-fighting heroes engaging in a fistfight with the supervillain's henchmen, and this is when the show's producers would paste pop art onto the TV screen, like Zap! and Pow!

Most leaders would love to infuse some zap and pow into their team. Well, it turns out that one of the big benefits to a clearly articulated and communicated purpose is em*power*ed people. And empowered people are connected to their organization's purpose and enjoy meaningful work.

In addition to empowering your people, having a clear organizational purpose has at least two more powerful benefits.

1. Intentionality

Successful organizations are intentional. When a worthy leader lives out a worthy cause (purpose) and consistently communicates that purpose, people in the organization get really intentional. When they clearly understand why they're pursuing the strategies, tactics, and performance goals they're responsible for, they can make every action count with their time and talent.

This kind of intentionality also empowers your people to govern themselves. They put team accomplishment ahead of what they can accomplish personally, sacrificing personal goals. It sets clear boundary lines for decision making, and your employees won't be overwhelmed or distracted by the constant change going on at warp-speed all around them in the workplace, the marketplace, and even their personal lives. They'll have more clarity about what to do and when to do it.

> *He who has a why to live for can bear almost any how.*
> —FRIEDRICH NIETZSCHE

2. Profits

Even though, according to Collins and Porras's definition, the purpose of a company is beyond just making money, purpose-driven companies usually make more money than more purely profit-driven companies.

In *Built to Last*, Collins and Porras dig into the historical performance of hundreds of the United States' most successful corporations, many dating back to the 1800s. Here is their conclusion:

> *Paradoxically, the visionary companies make more money than the more purely profit-driven companies.*

In his search to understand what created "visionary" organizations, they placed each company into one of three categories:

1. *Great or visionary* (extraordinary, enduring companies)
2. *Good* (comparison companies that were in similar industries as the visionary companies but fell short of visionary companies)
3. *Average* (reflecting the stock market)

The authors contrasted the three types of companies by showing what one dollar invested on January 1, 1926, would grow to by December 31, 1990. Here's what they found:

Growth of $1 Invested
1926-1990

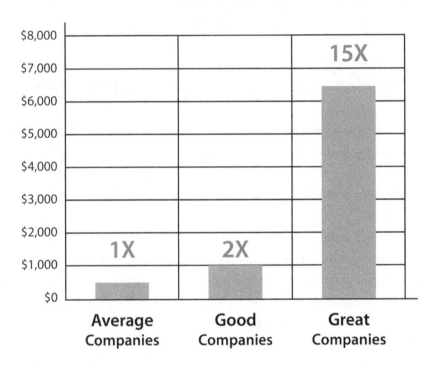

From 1926 to 1990, your investment in the good companies would have earned two times more than the general/average stock market—which is pretty good. But, your investment in the great, visionary companies would have been *fifteen times greater* than the average stock market.

Wow! So what made these great, visionary companies different? Collins and Porras discovered that the visionary companies did two things very well:

1. *Preserved the core*—the organizations' core ideology was fanatically protected and never changed.

2. *Stimulated progress*—by endlessly adapting their business and operating practices, they are driven by change, innovation, and improvement.

Over time, these visionary companies changed almost everything: policies, procedures, product lines, competencies, organizational structure, reward systems, strategies, tactics, and performance goals. But, the one thing that they did *not* change was their core ideology. And what do you think Collins and Porras defined as their *core ideology*? That equation is core values + purpose.

Shocking Fact: Visionary companies are generally more ideologically driven and less purely profit-driven.

I certainly saw the power of purpose in my own business. Prior to 2011, when I sold my business to a publicly traded company, my team and I knew we were doing meaningful work. At our company, our purpose was "Customers for Life." We worked hard—and in some cases, long—hours, but we had lots of fun in the process.

Why? Because we felt like we were part of something great—something greater than any one person. We enjoyed being part of a championship team. And we helped create a first-class culture—a culture where our people were not just committed to the leaders but, most of all, to each other, which led to a greater commitment to the company's purpose.

Now that I am living out my second half of life with my new business, Values-Driven Leadership, I'm doing my most meaningful work ever. I'm very focused on the right things, not the wrong things. I don't waste time on anything that doesn't fit my organization's purpose.

Not surprisingly, when we got crystal clear about who we were and why we existed, extraordinary results followed. Won't you consider tapping the power of purpose to propel your organization faster and further than the Dynamic Duo ever dreamed?

Take a True North Bearing

Do your people work hard and have fun doing so? What do you think about the most? What do you talk about the most with your employees? Have you considered a purpose-centered approach?

What Is a Purpose Statement?

Why does your business exist? What is your purpose?

In chapter 1, we cited Collins and Porras's definition of a purpose as our working definition: "the organization's fundamental reasons for existence beyond just making money."

Now let's take a deeper look at what a purpose statement is and what it is not.

A purpose statement is

- Authentic. This is key.
- A phrase of only a few words that is easy to remember.
- Broad, fundamental, and enduring. It should serve to guide and inspire the organization for years, perhaps a century or more, inspiring people to dream of doing great things.
- Never fully achieved or completed.
- Rock-solid and tightly fixed, which powerfully drives progress and enables the organization to change and adapt without compromising its purpose.
- Used to nurture and select senior management.

- Used to stir people to aspire to create something bigger and more lasting than themselves.
- Global. It can be exported regardless of which country the organization does business in.
- The corporate bonding glue where people's fundamental human need is met, which is to belong to something they can feel proud of.
- What makes people feel compelled to try to create greatness. It is something that you care so much about that you will want to make it the best it can possibly be, not because of what you will get but just because it can be done.
- A challenge for consistent alignment that gives guidance and inspiration to people inside the organization as they pursue strategies, tactics, goals, and organizational structures.
- As much to guide you on what activities *not* to pursue as it is to direct you toward those to pursue.

A purpose statement is not

- A description of how you are different from your competitors.
- Targeted to the financial community.
- Your product lines or customer segments.
- The "right" purpose statement. (There is no "right" purpose statement.)
- A description of how your organization fits the marketing trends and fashions of the day.
- A big program to induce radical change within the organization.

And, most importantly, a purpose statement is *not*

- Focused purely on shareholders' long-term wealth and profit maximization.

You may be thinking, "I don't have time for this stuff; I need my people to sell, sell, sell!" Well, you might have some good short-term results with that approach, but what we're talking about is intentional work that positions you and your organization to truly achieve lasting greatness.

Take a True North Bearing

Are you ready to put "power" in your people? Are you ready for your people to be intentional for a worthy cause beyond making money? Are you ready to discover your purpose for your organization?

Discover Your Organization's Purpose

Are you ready to have a purpose that strengthens your people's sense of unity and commitment as a team? Are you ready to create in your people's hearts and minds a frame of reference, a set of criteria or guidelines, by which they will govern themselves?

It is not enough to be industrious; so are the ants.
What are you industrious about?
—HENRY DAVID THOREAU

With the following six steps, you can draft a purpose statement for your employees, customers, and suppliers that clearly reflects why you exist.

1. Understand the criteria.

Before you draft your purpose statement, take a moment to review the section "What Is a Purpose Statement?" You must be clear about what a purpose statement is and what it isn't.

2. Determine your method.

Are you a one-man or one-woman show discovering the purpose for your startup company? Or, do you lead a team? Each scenario requires a different approach.

If you are a single employee in your business, you would go through this exercise alone or with a close and trusted friend or spouse.

If you are part of an organization with a team of employees and you have not created a purpose statement, the most effective way to have your people buy into it is to conduct a group exercise where your people are significantly involved in the creating process.

Where there's no involvement, there is no commitment.

And when you have no commitment, you will have a severe motivational problem that cannot be easily solved.

Will you be doing this process alone or with your team? Once you've answered that question, you can move on to number three.

3. Ask focusing questions.

Determining your organization's purpose requires some deep thinking. And there is nothing that stimulates thinking more than good questions. The following questions are designed to help you dig deeper into the meaning of why you exist. If you're the sole employee, you can answer these questions yourself or with a trusted partner; if you're leading a team, you can use these questions as the basis of your group exercise:

- Why does our organization exist?
- What motivates us to do the work that we do?
- What is the greatest possible impact we can make on the lives of others through our work?
- Why is this important?

To get the deepest answer, ask this last question a total of five times. This approach was made popular by the Toyota Motor Corporation to identify the root cause of a problem. It is a technique called "The Five Whys."[14] For example, if someone asked you, "Why does your organization exist?" what would you say? After thinking about your answer, if asked, "Why is that important?" what would you say next? If probed further and further, being asked again and again, "Why is that important?" what layers of purpose and meaning reveal themselves?

4. Aim for a bull's-eye single word.

Now, use the opposite approach, and ask yourself (or your people), "What single word is the bull's-eye of the bull's-eye, the focus of the focus, the center of the center, the very essence of our organization?" Even though this word is not your purpose statement, it is the essence, the single-word focus.

Simplicity produces clarity. Though the process of elimination to find that single word may take several attempts, that single word will turn everything you do into meaningful work—organizational meetings, projects, and employee, customer, and supplier relationships.

5. Prepare one simple phrase.

The next step is to ask, "Instead of having one word, what three words would you use to focus your energies on?" Now write a simple, nontechnical three-word phrase that everyone can clearly understand that becomes your purpose statement.

Refine your purpose statement so that when someone asks you what your organization is about, you can simply say, "The reason we exist is to . . ."

6. Validate your work.

Once you have discovered your organization's purpose, ask each individual involved in the process to independently answer the following questions with yes or no. These questions were compiled by best-selling author Jim Collins:

---

14   Courtney Seiter, "The Formula to Better Problem Solving," *Fast Company* (online), January 7, 2015, https://www.fastcompany.com/3040428/the-formula-to-better-problem-solving.

1. Do you find this purpose personally inspiring?

2. Can you envision this purpose being as valid 100 years from now as it is today?

3. Does the purpose help you think expansively about the long-term possibilities and range of activities the organization can consider over the next 100 years, beyond its current products, services, markets, industries, and strategies?

4. Does the purpose help you to decide what activities to not pursue, to eliminate from consideration?

5. Is this purpose authentic—something true to what the organization is all about—not merely words on paper that "sound nice"?

6. Would this purpose be greeted with enthusiasm rather than cynicism by a broad base of people in the organization?

7. When telling your children and/or other loved ones what you do for a living, would you feel proud in describing your work in terms of this purpose?[15]

If most of your people (at least 80 to 90 percent) answer yes to all of the questions above, then you can confidently move forward with your new purpose statement. If not, then you need to keep working through the process until you have widespread alignment around these questions.

To download my Discovery Guide for Your Organization's Purpose, which includes all these questions, go to TNB-book.com.

---

15 "Vision Framework," JimCollins.com, https://www.jimcollins.com/tools/vision-framework. pdf.

Take a True North Bearing

Have you discovered your organization's purpose? Have you arranged for your people as a team to help you discover your purpose?

Defining the purpose of your organization is hard work, but the results are worth it.

Average companies give their people something to work on. In contrast, the most innovative organizations give their people something to work toward.
—SIMON SINEK

Now that you've discovered why you exist, it's time to discover where you are going. That brings us to the topic of the next two chapters: discovering your vision.

CHAPTER 10

Do You Know Where You Are Going?

If You Don't Know Where You're Going, You'll Never Get There

Vision is the art of seeing what is invisible to others.
—JONATHAN SWIFT

The other day, two of my young grandkids (they call me G-Bob for Grand-Bob) wanted me to fly the paper airplanes they had made. It reminded me of when I was their age and my mom and dad would take me with them every Friday night to their couples bowling league. As you can imagine, being a high-energy boy, I was bored stiff. That is, until I would find a piece of paper and, with a few simple folds, transform it into a plane.

Think back to your younger years when you made paper airplanes and tossed them into the air again and again. When the planes took flight, where did they land? You never knew what their flight path would be, did you?

I remember sometimes my planes made a full circle and went straight to the floor. Other times, they would gently glide across the bowling house until hitting someone with surprise. That's when I would go hide, like nothing had happened.

You know, we do not arrive at our desired destination in life and in business by accident. If we don't know where we're going, we tend to drift away from our dreams.

> *If you could get all the people in the organization rowing in the same direction, you could dominate any industry, in any market, against any competition, at any time.*
> —PATRICK LENCIONI

If you have no vision, you also will never arrive at your desired destination. Why? There is a law at work in the natural world that is also operative in your life and business: the second law of thermodynamics. This principle tells us that the physical world is decaying and that the direction of all creation is downward, not upward. Everything eventually runs down.

Have you ever wondered why a garden left untended eventually becomes overgrown with weeds? The answer is that everything in the natural world is decaying. And if we do not exert a proactive countereffort, the natural course of events will lead us to drift, like a paper airplane, in both life and business. That is why it is essential to develop a vision statement to reverse the natural tendency toward drift and decline.

My good friend and mentor Jim Lundy reminded me of this tendency with these wise words:

If you don't know where you are going,

. . . any path will get you there,

. . . but you won't realize if you're lost,

. . . you won't know what time you'll arrive,

. . . you won't know the dimensions of your challenge,

. . . others won't understand how they could help,

. . . and since you could pass right by without recognizing it,

. . . you won't get the satisfaction of having arrived.

I learned early in life that it was important for me to pause, reflect, and plan so I could know where I was going. But, I also learned that it was even more important to clarify the vision—where I was going in the workplace—so we would all go down the right road together.

Likewise, in your personal life and with your workplace team, you can reach your destination much sooner by avoiding an ambiguous vision.

An Ambiguous Vision

Consider the following example, which illustrates the adverse effects of an ambiguous vision.

Imagine that you are at a family reunion picnic, and you decide to try your hand at a game of archery. You select your bow and receive as many arrows as you wish. As you step up to the line, you notice there is no target in sight.

Then someone who is overseeing the game says, "Okay, select an arrow, draw your bow, and shoot!"

What do you do next? Do you just stand there waiting for further instructions? With no defined target, I bet you would hesitate to draw your bow. But, let's say you shoot one arrow just to see what happens. If you shoot, you would learn what it feels like when you do not know where the target is.

Without the feedback of seeing how close you came to the target, you could not adjust your aim in order to hit closer to the bull's-eye next time—because there is no bull's-eye! You would have no way of knowing if you came close to hitting the target. In other words, you could not gauge your level of success.

An ambiguous vision without adequate feedback, in your personal life and in the workplace, will lead to confusion and frustration.

Achievement and recognition are two of the best motivators. And for our personal life and as leaders, we should provide ourselves, as well as our employees, with a chance to seek and achieve fulfillment in endeavors.

But first, the vision of where you are going must be clearly defined, understood, and accepted as reasonable to be fully beneficial. Your personal life and your workplace employees need a vision for the future so actions can be corrected when targets are missed and so everyone can feel the deserved satisfaction when targets are hit.

Take a True North Bearing

Are you drifting like a paper airplane? Would you like a sense of personal and work achievement and the recognition for that achievement?

Why Some People Almost Never Know Where They Are Going

A few years ago, my wife and I enjoyed a day at Walt Disney World with one of our sons, our daughter-in-law, and our two young grandkids. I especially remember riding the Prince Charming Regal Carrousel with our two grandkids.

We all got situated on the ride, and when that merry-go-round started, those kids cracked a really big smile. And that smile lasted until . . . the merry-go-round stopped, and it was time for us to dismount our magnificent horses. Then the crying started, their bottom lips pushed outward, and we had to carry them off the merry-go-round.

Aren't we at times like my grandkids when we become addicted to short-term pleasure and gratification? When it stops, we not only want it again, but want it to come quickly and more powerfully than before. Then, when we don't get what we want, we cry out and blame someone or something else.

As we discussed in chapter 2, people who behave expediently do what's easiest and quickest or what makes them the happiest in the short run. They tend to make emotional decisions that are reactive in nature.

People who behave in an expedient way find it more convenient to react to the urgent things in life and in business. They are often guided by emotion and choose to make popular decisions that are rooted in unhealthy fears. At the same time, they worry about protecting their rights. But, sadly, emotional decisions made in haste lead to poor outcomes.

They pour so much energy and effort into their short-term emotions that they tend to lose sight of the long-term—where they are going—their vision.

Would you like to get off this life that has been like a merry-go-round? You can stop going around in circles by changing how you think.

In chapter 3, we talked about the importance of changing how we think as part of the ON/IN leadership practice. In his classic book *As a Man Thinketh*, James Allen states, "A man is literally what he thinks, his character being the complete sum of all his thoughts."[16] That can either be a good thing or a bad thing.

One of the reasons people don't achieve their dreams is that they desire to change their results (in an expedient way) without changing their thinking. You can only begin making principled, proactive, and character-driven decisions to determine where you are going—your vision—when you change your thinking.

As you continue the thought changing process, it is important to remember that . . .

We make choices, and our choices make us.

- You are responsible for your own choices, and you have the freedom to choose how you respond to what you experience in life.
- You can change (if you are willing and have the desire) how you think about making choices, which leads to more right decisions.
- You can change where you spend your time and energy by focusing more on what you *can* control and less on what you *cannot* control.

---

16 James Allen, *As a Man Thinketh* (CreateSpace, 2006).

Take a True North Bearing

Has your life been like riding a merry-go-round? Are you
ready to change how you think?

An Abundance Mindset: The Secret to Discovering Your Vision

I was saddened to hear of a talented athlete who was recently featured in the national news for unlawful conduct (again). So much talent under so little control. A couple of years ago, he seemed destined to live out a hall-of-fame-level career, but now he's headed nowhere—and fast. His vision for the future is looking pretty bleak.

As leaders, we will all make mistakes—maybe even some big ones. The real question is, what will we do next? The answer to that question is determined by your mindset. We can change our mindset by changing our thinking.

When I was a young boy, starting in junior high school and through college, I worked with my dad's moving crews. I took on being the "swampier" for the crews. I did the work the others did not want to do or did not like to do. I took one break from work to their two. (The crew often would kid me that they were taking a chewing gum break because I did not smoke.) I also would run or walk fast between the house and the truck, passing them as they walked. But why?

When I was in high school and in college, I always did the extra credit work, not because I needed the extra grade (I usually already had an A in the class). But why?

When my dad suddenly died and I became the boss at twenty years old, I would fall asleep most nights diligently studying about our industry and trends in other industries. But why?

Somehow, I just knew that through all of the times I gave this extra effort, I was developing and building my character—who I was *becoming*. I approached life with an abundance mindset, and I knew that, personally, I had room to grow.

When I look over my life, I don't have any regrets. Have I made mistakes? Yes. Have I ever been very disappointed? Yes. Still, somehow, I have always learned from my mistakes, overcome disappointments, and moved forward. Even if I make a mistake, instead of dwelling on it, my thinking usually goes to considering my next options.

Over the many years I've been in business and worked closely with other leaders, I've seen that the most successful ones have the same abundance mindset. In fact, I believe there's a direct connection between your ability to be a visionary leader and having an abundance mindset. It's the secret sauce to dreaming big, getting where you want to go, and helping the most people along the way.

It all goes back to the Path of Effective Leadership concept of principle vs. expediency. As you may remember from chapter 2, principled leaders tend to have an abundance mindset, while expedient leaders tend to have a scarcity mindset.

An abundance mindset enables you to set and achieve your greatest vision.

A scarcity mindset will limit your ability to even set a vision. You may ask, "Why is that so?" I believe it is because people with a scarcity mindset never let go of what they have, and when you don't let go of what you have, you can never fully reach out for and grab hold of a greater vision of what could be.

People with a scarcity mindset think short term while people with an abundance mindset think long term about where they are going. They have a clear vision, which means they're much more likely to achieve it.

People with an abundance mindset believe that today's short-term pain, sacrifice, and investment in time, energy, and money will eventually bring long-term growth, blessings, and success. And they are more likely to get where they are going and achieve their vision. People who adopt an abundance mindset approach life, challenges, and opportunities in a principled manner and with a grateful heart, which literally paves the way for them to succeed.

Take a True North Bearing

Do you want long-term growth, blessings, and success? Are you willing to accept short-term sacrifice?

How to Develop an Abundance Mindset

Do you have an abundance mindset or a scarcity mindset? Every person can develop an abundance mindset by adopting the following five attributes.

1. Understand there is enough.

Abundant thinkers know there is enough in the world for everyone to share in a piece of the pie. They understand that the more you share in a principled way, the more the abundance grows.

Scarcity thinkers believe there is not enough of anything to go around. They fear that there will not be enough for them, especially if they share with others.

2. Give time, talent, and treasures.

Abundant thinkers know that when they give their time, talent, and treasures, these will come back to them, thus increasing the abundance in their own lives. This principled process strengthens and fosters team building and creative thinking, which support continual improvement in the workplace.

Scarcity thinkers do not share. After all, they are driven by a deep-seated belief that there isn't enough to go around, so they cannot afford to give anything away. They truly believe that if they share their knowledge or wealth, they will lose power and possessions both now and in the future.

The freedom and success enjoyed by abundant thinkers becomes obvious when we contrast it with the limiting beliefs of scarcity thinkers.

Scarcity thinking weakens our effectiveness and keeps us from realizing our full potential. But, a perspective of abundance ensures that there's always enough to go around and keeps us moving forward.

3. Don't compare.

Abundant thinkers don't compare themselves with others—only with themselves. They set realistic goals and then work to achieve them. They encourage others to do the same. Their goals are based (in a principled way) upon a logical study of achievable results in each step.

Scarcity thinkers continually ask themselves why they aren't like others or why they do not have the things others have. If others are younger or prettier or more handsome, then others are perceived to have an advantage. In the workplace, these types of supervisors lead by keeping their workers subservient, since equality would be viewed as competition.

4. Think win/win.

Abundant thinkers find common ground with their colleagues. They know that unresolved conflict is wasted time and energy and subtracts from an abundant environment. They see win/win and assume that there is a way for all concerned to profit and thrive. They understand that constructive criticism helps others to grow.

Scarcity thinkers want to be at the center of attention because they want all they can get for themselves. They know (sometimes unconsciously) that for this to happen, others have to lose. They think that if they can use expedient means to get something done more quickly, their win justifies their survival-of-the-fittest approach.

5. Embrace gratitude.

Abundant thinkers live lives of gratitude for the abundance of the world in which they live. They are positive and upbeat. To them, life is a continuously replenished bowl of fruit—all ripe for the taking. They teach others how to be positive and live in gratitude.

Scarcity thinkers are not grateful for what they have. They see their life's accomplishments as the result of only their hard work and are unable to give heartfelt thanks to others for helping. In the workplace, scarcity thinkers teach their followers that life's abundance is limited and they had better do what they need to do to grab the brass ring.

You, too, regardless of age, have room to grow personally, which affects who you are becoming. And when you do, you will have an abundance mindset that will help you see where you are going—your vision.

Take a True North Bearing

Are you open to personal growth? What challenge or opportunity are you facing today that would benefit from a shift toward greater abundance thinking?

Are you ready to discover where you are going? Just as you need a life purpose and an organizational purpose, so, too, you need a personal vision and an organizational vision. Once again, we'll start with you first.

CHAPTER 11

Determine Your Personal Vision

Stop Drifting and Define Your Destination

> *When you have vision it affects your attitude. Your attitude is optimistic rather than pessimistic.*
> —CHARLES R. SWINDOLL

We all are climbing a ladder in life. And there are lots of ladders. You know what is amazing? If our ladder is not leaning against the right wall, then every step we take just gets us to the wrong place faster.

In your personal life, you may be very busy being efficient, but without a vision, you will not be effective in achieving your goals. You may be climbing the wrong ladder, and you may not realize it until you're at the top and it's too late to climb another.

> *It's incredibly easy to get caught up in an activity trap, in the busy-ness of life, to work harder and harder at climbing the ladder of success only to discover it's leaning against the wrong wall. It is possible to be busy—very busy—without being very effective.*
> —STEPHEN R. COVEY

Stephen R. Covey tells us when you "begin with the end in mind" (your vision), you can make certain that you do not violate your principles. This approach positions you to correctly deal with your problems and contribute each day in a meaningful way. It ensures you're climbing the right ladder—and if you're not, it helps you course-correct as early as possible.

What Is a Vision Statement?

Before you begin writing your vision statement, it's important to know exactly what it is.

Note: the criteria below apply to both a personal vision statement and an organizational vision statement, which we'll cover in the next chapter.

Let's first start with what a vision statement is *not*. It is not

- About money. Money only gets temporary movement; it is not enough to actually motivate you. You will work harder for meaning than for money.
- Verbose
- Hard to understand and convoluted
- Impossible to remember

Instead, a vision statement

- Preserves your core values and purpose (which never change) and stimulates progress (which is always changing)
- Is vibrant and engaging
- Produces a visual image or picture
- Is a huge, daunting, exhilarating challenge
- Is clear and compelling
- Is something people "get" right away
- Serves as a focal point
- Galvanizes people
- Catalyzes and creates a team spirit as people strive toward it (if an organization)

- Inspires passion, intensity, emotion, and conviction for living it out
- Has a wow factor, where you would feel fantastic if you could make it happen
- Is something you really want to be a part of and are willing to put significant effort into realizing
- Energizes and excites you
- Will require a quantum step forward in your capabilities and characteristics
- Is something you are 100 percent committed to

Preparing to Determine Your Personal Vision

As we begin this process, I'm reminded of the following story. A traveling salesman was lost, driving down a quiet country road. When he saw a young boy walking toward him, he slowed down, stopped, and called to the boy, "Where am I?"

"There you are," said the boy as he pointed at the man.

"Hey, you're pretty stupid, aren't you?" said the upset driver.

"Well, you're the one asking the dumb questions!" replied the kid.

My good friend and mentor Jim Lundy told me that story to emphasize that before you can know where you are going, you must first ask yourself two questions. To help you prepare for writing your personal vision statement, I invite you to answer those same two questions:

1. Where have you been?
2. Where are you now?

Write Your Personal Vision Statement

Once you know where you've been and where you are, you're ready to answer the question, where are you going? The answer to this question is your personal vision statement. You can cast a vision by following these two simple steps.

1. Thoroughly understand the criteria.

Before you draft your vision statement, take a moment to review the previous section "What Is a Vision Statement?" so you're clear about what a vision statement is and what it isn't.

2. Vividly describe your vision.

Use words to clearly describe your personal vision so that you can explain it to other people.

Here's one way you can capture your vision in sufficient detail. Vividly describe your accomplishments as though you have been asked to write an article fifteen years from now for an international publication about an award you have received for accomplishing your personal vision. Consider the following questions:

- What has been your unique impact on the people in your circle of influence?
- How do your closest friends describe their friendship with you? What makes them say wow about your relationship with them?
- What has this achievement meant to you?
- How have you grown personally and what competencies have you developed?
- What are family, friends, and coworkers saying about your accomplishments? Why?

Based on your answers to questions above, what *must* you do? What is your desired destination in life? What does this destination look like in detail? Where are you going? This is your personal vision.

If you'd like a worksheet to determine your personal vision, go to TNB-book.com to download my Personal Vision-Casting Worksheet.

What would you attempt to do
if you knew you could not fail?
—ROBERT H. SCHULLER

As you will find, personal vision statements are exactly that: personal. Mine is deeply rooted in my spiritual beliefs. Yours may be, too—or not at all. Also, please note that vision statements can change over time. I have found it rare, however, for purpose statements to change.

As owner of the Albert Companies, for a long time, my personal vision was wrapped up in our company's vision statement. However, over time, I began to realize my personal vision: "Encourage people to integrate the lordship of Jesus Christ into every area of their life."

Take a True North Bearing

Do you know where you are personally going in life? When can you set aside time in your schedule this week to work on your personal vision?

You can reach your destination much sooner if you know where you're going. What is true for you personally is also true for your business. Successful people know where they are going. And they have a plan for getting there. You'll learn how to determine your organization's vision in the next chapter.

CHAPTER 12

Determine Your Organization's Vision

Unify Your Team around a Clear Vision

Chase the vision, not the money.
The money will end up following you.
—TONY HSIEH

My long-time friend and mentor Jim Lundy and I would often talk about how managing a business was more like following a winding road rather than a straight path. Despite our best efforts to head straight to our destination (our vision), we still tended to "zig and zag" back and forth as we moved forward.

In chapter 2, "The Path of Effective Leadership," we discussed the importance of both leading *and* managing. But, there is a proper order. It was my responsibility to first lead our people (enhance relationships) before I managed the things of our business (pursued results).

The Business Two-Step

According to author Stephen R. Covey in *The 7 Habits of Highly Effective People*

- Leadership is about *effectiveness*. It asks the question, "What are the things I want to accomplish?" It determines whether the ladder is leaning against the right wall.
- Management is about *efficiency*. It asks the question, "How can I best accomplish certain things?" It's busy climbing the ladder of success.

> *Management is doing things right;*
> *leadership is doing the right things.*
> —Peter Drucker

Stephen Covey commented that *managers* (the producers, the problem solvers) are the ones cutting their way through the jungle. They are the ones sharpening their machetes, writing policy and procedure manuals, holding muscle development programs, bringing in improved technologies, and setting up working schedules and compensation programs.

The *leader* is the one who climbs the tallest tree, surveys the entire situation, and yells, "Wrong jungle!" But how do the busy, efficient producers and managers often respond? "Shut up! We're making progress."

As individuals, groups, and businesses, we're often so busy cutting through the undergrowth we don't even realize we're in the wrong jungle. Yet, the rapidly changing environment in which we live makes effective leadership more critical than ever before.

> *No management success can compensate*
> *for failure in leadership.*
> —Stephen R. Covey

Effective leaders need a vision (a destination) and their core values and purpose (a compass) to guide them. We often don't know what the terrain ahead will be like or what we will need to go through it; much will depend on our judgment at the time.

Effective leadership—and even our survival—does not depend solely on how much effort we expend but on whether or not the effort we expend is in the right jungle.

Proactive leadership must constantly monitor environmental change, particularly customer buying habits and motives, and provide the force necessary to organize resources in the right direction. Leadership needs to keep everyone headed in the right direction. Why? Because there is no amount of management expertise that can keep the team from failing.

Parents are also trapped in the management paradigm, thinking of control, efficiency, and rules instead of direction, purpose, and family feelings.

Leadership is even more lacking in our personal lives. We tend to manage with efficiency by setting and achieving goals before we have even clarified our values (Who am I?) and our purpose (Why do I exist?).

Every person can minimize triangulation in life and in business by doing two things and doing them in order.

1. Lead first.

You are responsible for leading yourself personally first with a vision, and as the leader of your business, for leading your people first with a vision (a destination, a direction, a dream) as to where you are going.

Leadership is the capacity to translate vision into reality.
—WARREN BENNIS

2. Manage second.

You are responsible for pausing, reflecting, thinking, and evaluating/managing your progress toward your vision for yourself personally and for your business.

Plan your work and work your plan.
—NAPOLEON HILL

I have observed that when we jump first to solve a problem before we have a vision (a direction), we immediately place a ceiling on our personal and business growth.

Do you find yourself triangulating here and then there, back and forth, and making little headway? If so, could I suggest that you take the two simple (but not easy) steps above? Lead first, manage second, and then watch what happens.

We Texans know how to two-step on the dance floor, but I've discovered a Business Two-Step that will help you "cut a rug" in life and business. Create your vision first and help your people get there second.

Take a True North Bearing

In your life and business, do you lead first,
before you start managing?

Four Important Leadership Qualities

Just as leaders are responsible for clarifying their personal vision, they're also responsible for clarifying and communicating the vision of their organization, division, or department. It's part of leading first and managing second. If you don't know where you are going, you shouldn't be surprised if you end up where you don't want to be.

But the same prerequisite needed for knowing and sharing your organization's purpose is also required for your organization's vision. You must first be a trustworthy leader. All leaders can successfully achieve their vision by living out the following four leadership qualities.

1. Trust

We covered this in chapter 9 but it's worth covering again. Remember, trust is the foundation of leadership. If your people trust you, they'll forgive occasional mistakes, but if you break their trust, you forfeit your ability to lead. Remember, you can earn your people's respect by displaying these qualities:

- Integrity
- Humility
- Authenticity
- Selflessness

Also, leaders must first believe in their people before their people will believe in them.

2. Connection

Connection occurs when you win people over before you enlist their help. You, as the leader, have the responsibility to initiate connection with your people.

Never underestimate the power of building relationships with your people before asking them to follow you.

> *To lead yourself, use your head, to lead others, use your heart. Always touch a person's heart before you ask him for a hand.*
> —John Maxwell

When the leader has done well connecting with his people, such as through the process of MBWA (Management by Walking Around—see chapter 2), you can expect to see employees exhibiting loyalty and a strong work ethic. And the leader's vision becomes an inspiration for the people.

3. Empowerment

When you, as the leader, use group exercises to brainstorm ideas and thoughts and when you sincerely seek your people's input, your people have a better understanding of and commitment to the decision that you collaboratively make.

Furthermore, when employees are involved in the creation and implementation planning stages, they take pride in the achievement of the decisions that help reach the vision, the dream.

4. Navigation

Good leaders do more than control the direction in which they and their people travel. They also

- See the whole trip in their mind before moving forward.
- Have a vision for getting to their destination.
- Understand what it will take to get there.
- Know who they'll need on the team to be successful.
- Recognize the obstacles long before they appear.

A leader is one who sees more than others see, who sees farther than others see, and who sees before others do.
—LeRoy Eims

Leaders who effectively navigate have the ability to balance between

- Optimism and realism
- Intuition and planning
- Faith and fact

And they have a professional will to find a way for the team to succeed because they believe that anything less than success is unacceptable.

It is *not* the size of the vision or project that determines success. It is the size of the leader.

Anyone can steer the ship, but it takes
a leader to chart the course.
—JOHN MAXWELL

Take a True North Bearing

Are you being the leader required for your team's success? Which leadership quality listed above could you improve upon?

Preparing to Write Your Organizational Vision Statement

For ten years straight, I organized a canoe trip for a group of guys. We had fun times paddling down the Guadalupe River in the Hill Country of Central Texas. The Guadalupe is the most popular canoeing river in the state and offers some of the most advanced canoeing in the United States.

The river boasts several stretches of white water rapids, and life preservers should be worn at all times, especially at the Waco Springs and Slumber Falls sections where many lives are lost each year.

My brother-in-law and I always partnered, and he invariably wanted me to be at the rear of the canoe. I think it was because I developed an ability to look down the river, use my paddle to power us faster than the speed of the water flow, and steer the canoe in the best direction.

If you allow the river's water flow to exceed the speed of your canoe, you can easily lose control of your canoe, making it likely you'll hit a hazard and capsize. As you can imagine, there are many hazards as you journey down the

Guadalupe's twists and turns, and you have to expect to get wet when (not if) your canoe capsizes.

The same principle applies to business. If the marketplace (water flow) is traveling faster than your business, your business will eventually fail (capsize).

Despite the many challenges that occurred during these canoe trips, we were confident of one thing: we were going to reach our destination, our shared vision. But, we couldn't just jump in the canoe and head down the river. To actually arrive at our destination, we had to plan first.

Since the leadership of these trips fell to me, I would schedule fun pre-meetings full of "war stories" and "heroics" to set the dates. I prepared a checklist of all the things I had to organize and complete before the trip (e.g., receive canoe deposits from each person, reserve canoes and hotel rooms, get laminated river maps, etc.) and a checklist of what each person needed for the trip.

You know that leading a business is much like leading an adventurous journey with many twists and turns. There are hazards, obstacles, and boulders that challenge you to navigate around and through them as you move forward to your destination, your vision. And I have discovered that just as with a canoe trip, *preparation* is the key to success.

> *There is no shortcut to achievement. Life requires thorough preparation—veneer isn't worth anything.*
> —GEORGE WASHINGTON CARVER

As leaders, we need to take certain steps to prepare for this important process of discovering our organizational vision. Every leader can prepare to write a vision statement by taking three steps. If you remember the principle of goals and controls from "The Path of Effective Leadership" in chapter 2, you'll find this process familiar.

1. Ask

As we explained in chapter 11, in the process of determining your personal vision, before you can know where you are going, you must first ask yourself two questions:

1. Where have you been?
2. Where are you now?

2. Connect: MBWA

After you've answered those two key questions, the next step in preparing to write your vision is to connect with your people. One of the best ways to connect with your people is to regularly do MBWA (see chapter 2).

If you ask questions and listen, the responses will be amazing. People will become energized simply because you asked.

3. Analyze: SWOT

The final step is to do a SWOT analysis. A SWOT analysis is a structured planning method used to find your competitive advantage by evaluating the internal factors and external factors of the organization.

You may ask, what do all these questions have to do with discovering your vision? Let me share with you how they helped us. For many years prior to selling my company in 2011, as a result of regularly working ON the business, I was an avid student of trends inside the moving and storage industry and other industries as well. This habit allowed me to develop a keen perspective on external opportunities, threats, and trends. Ultimately, this practice allowed us to discover our vision statement.

My company had just gone through a successful quality improvement exercise where we gained hundreds and hundreds of ideas to improve service to our customers. And we were rolling out a new, innovative business offering from my moving and storage company.

One day, a good friend of mine, who was consulting with us on this new business offering, very calmly said, "We are revolutionizing the way people move."

I immediately said, "That is it!"

And he looked at me like, "What is it?"

I said, "That is our vision statement: Revolutionizing the Way People Move!"

Again, it was a process, not an event. The three steps I described above occurred over a period of weeks, months, and even years as I was investing time working ON my business. If I had not spent a lengthy amount of time on this process (or tried to skip or shortcut it), I would not have so quickly recognized my friend's words as our vision statement.

Take a True North Bearing

Does your organization have a vision statement? Do you have the passion and the faith that you will prevail in the end as you confront the most brutal facts of your current reality?

Determine Your Organization's Vision

So how about you? Have you thought about the future of your organization? Where would you like it to be in five, ten, or even thirty years?

All leaders can determine their organization's vision by following three simple steps.

1. Thoroughly understand the criteria.

Earlier, we talked about what a vision statement is and what it's not. Take a moment to review the section "What Is a Vision Statement?" in chapter 11.

2. Vividly describe your vision.

Use words to clearly describe your vision so that you and your employees can explain it to all stakeholders (e.g., employees, customers, suppliers, investors). Your envisioned future should be so vivid to you that it's as if you've already taken the journey and you're coming back to take your people up to the mountain top so they can experience the same victory.

One way to do this is to use a variation of the exercise recommended in chapter 11, "Write Your Personal Vision." In that exercise, I asked you to write an article vividly describing your personal accomplishments fifteen years from now and provided leading questions. Here I ask you to do the same, but in this article, describe the accomplishments of your company or organization fifteen years from now. Here are some questions to consider:

- What has been your unique impact on the marketplace?
- What are your customers experiencing? Why are they saying "wow!" to describe your service?
- What have these achievements meant to your employees? How do they feel?
- What competencies and systems have you developed?
- What are your suppliers saying about your accomplishments? And why?

3. Collaboratively record your vision.

After you have reviewed the criteria and written a vivid description of your ideal future as an empowering leader, you should involve and seek input from your employees. It is important to ask for this input at the very beginning of the casting-a-vision-statement process (see above) and before stating the final version of the vision statement. A good way to determine whom to include in this process is to ask yourself these three key questions, which you'll learn more about in part 4:

1. *Who* can help me write a better vision statement?
2. *Who* will have to carry it out?
3. *Who* will be impacted by it?

Then involve those people by using group exercises to brainstorm two, three, or five snippets from the vivid description. When you sincerely seek your people's input, your people have a better understanding of and commitment to the vision you collaboratively set.

Furthermore, when employees are involved in the development/creation of a clear, concise vision statement, they take pride in the achievement of the vision.

If you'd like to use a worksheet to determine your personal vision, go to TNB-book.com to download my Organizational Vision-Casting Worksheet.

Take a True North Bearing

What is your destiny? Is now the time to clearly define your
vision and ask your people to help?

I have another question for you. Have you figured out why part 3 of this book is called "WOW!"? The first W is your *why* (purpose), the O has no meaning, and the second W is your *where* (vision).

After you complete the process in chapters 9 and 12 to discover your organization's WOW!, it is time for you to have a celebration announcement and begin to put it into practice.

CHAPTER 13

Roll Out Your Organization's WOW!

A Communication Plan That Produces Passion and Buy-In

The single biggest problem in communication is the illusion that it has taken place.
—GEORGE BERNARD SHAW

As leaders, once we discover our organization's WOW!, the next logical step is to spread the word.

My pulse quickens and I can feel the excitement build within me when I think about a leader effectively communicating his purpose and vision to his team. And even though it can be challenging, the rewards are worth it. But, it takes much more than the leader just announcing the purpose and vision. Let me take you back in time and share how we did it at my moving and storage company.

WOW! QIC Day

Every year for nine years, our business held a half-day, company-wide meeting we called QIC Day (pronounced *quick*, which stands for Quality Is

Contagious). The purpose of a QIC Day was to emphasize a yearly theme. The theme of the meeting after we finalized our vision statement was WOW! And, I could hardly wait!

Years prior to our WOW! QIC Day, our people had already heard me speak about our purpose (Customers for Life) and our vision (Revolutionizing the Way People Move). The WOW! QIC Day would help us further codify our thinking about the WOW! concepts:

W Why do we exist? (our purpose)
O (has no meaning)
W Where are we going? (our vision)

Plan for Fun

I have found that interactive group activities are the best way to help folks dive deeper into any topic. Plus, research shows that if people are having the right kind of fun, they learn and retain better.

So, we intentionally planned such activities for this important day. As our employees arrived for our WOW! QIC Day, we asked them to sit at preassigned table groups of no more than eight people per table. This group size, we reasoned, would help employees:

- Engage in interaction and discussion
- Enjoy the games we were about to compete in

Our decision to use assigned seating was intentional. In any organization, I have found people rarely talk to those outside their small group of friends or to people in other departments. In my company, for example, people in the office rarely spoke with the moving crews. When we assigned seating, our objective was to get people to have fun and start discussions with those they typically didn't talk to. It was amazing how people in the office were so surprised by how smart the people on the moving crews were. And everyone developed new friends at work.

Each game played was designed to allow our people to:

- Have fun

- Learn to work as a team
- Discover practical applications

Game #1: To kick off the meeting, we used an icebreaker game that required everyone to get up and move across the room to ask assigned questions to learn something personal about someone they didn't know before.

Game #2: I'm sure you've heard of Monopoly, the classic family board game. Well, we played a similar game. Since we were in the moving and storage business, we called our custom-made board game Moveopoly. We created the board ahead of time, and as part of the day's activities, each table created their own game cards based on their actual responses to our purpose and vision. You'll learn more about how we did this later in the chapter. (I still have the original custom game board template we made.)

Clarify the Message: Purpose

At our WOW! QIC Day, we divided our agenda into two parts:

1. Our purpose
2. Our vision

First, let's look at how I rolled out and communicated our purpose. I began by reminding everyone that our organization's purpose, the reason why we exist, is to create Customers for Life. I also shared with our people our three priorities related to this purpose:

1. Grow business in existing markets
2. Expand business into compatible niche markets
3. Develop and sustain long-term customer relationships

Afterwards, we had open discussions about what these three priorities looked like for our business specifically.

Amplify the Awareness: Purpose

During the meeting, we used two questions to stimulate thinking and discussion about our purpose (why we exist):

1. Can you identify the things that delight (not just satisfy) our customers and achieve our purpose, Customers for Life? (positive thoughts)
2. Can you identify the things that turn customers off? (negative thoughts)

I used the following process to engage our people to participate in the facilitation exercise about our purpose:

- I introduced the first of the purpose-related questions from above and asked our people to discuss at their table possible answers to that question.
- Next, each table used their flip chart to record their ideas and answers in response to the first question.
- Then, one-by-one, each table was asked to share their best idea for that question with the entire group.
- Then, we repeated the process for the second question.

Finally, after the process was completed for both questions, we all played the Moveopoly board game about our purpose. Each table created their own game cards based on the answers shared as part of the previous exercise. Cards were made using the ten positive thoughts and ten negative thoughts our people gave during the facilitation exercise.

Boy, did our people have lots of fun playing Moveopoly and competing against the other table teams for special prizes. But, most of all, while they were having a ball and using the positive cards and negative cards containing their own thoughts, the game completely reinforced how they were going to achieve our purpose of Customers for Life.

Take a True North Bearing

How could you use a similar game-based discovery approach with your people to deeply communicate your message to them? If such an approach improved the attitudes and cohesiveness of your team, how valuable would that be to your organization and your leadership effectiveness?

Clarify the Message: Vision

Next, it was time to roll out and communicate our vision. I shared our vision of where we were going: Revolutionizing the Way People Move. I also shared our three priorities in getting there:

1. Develop value-adding services responsive to customers' wants and needs.
2. Develop innovative processes to fulfill customer wants and needs.
3. Consistently deliver a service experience that exceeds customers' expectations.

Afterwards, we had open discussions as to what these three priorities specifically looked like for our business.

Amplify the Awareness: Vision

Then, we used two discussion questions to stimulate thinking and discussion about our vision:

1. What attitudes, behaviors, or actions will enhance and promote progress toward our vision? (positive thoughts)

2. What factors will hinder or limit our efforts to progress toward our vision? (negative thoughts)

Just as I did with our purpose, I used the following process to lead our people to participate in the facilitation exercise about our vision:

- I introduced the first of the vision-related questions from above and asked our people to discuss at their table possible answers to that question.
- Next, each table used its flip chart to record ideas and answers in response to the first question.
- One by one, each table was asked to share its best idea for that question with the entire group.
- Then we repeated the process for the second question.

Finally, we all played the Moveopoly board game again, this time focusing on our vision, using cards made from the positive thoughts (that contributed to our progress) and the negative thoughts (that set us back) our people gave during the facilitation exercise. Once again, everyone had fun while our vision of Revolutionizing the Way People Move was reinforced.

Take a True North Bearing

Do you know where you have been and where are you now? Do you know where you are going as an organization? How might you use a game-based approach to share this with your organization?

WOW!: Essential for Transformation

Do you want change—or even transformation—to happen in your organization? Transformation occurs only when your people actually live and behave differently than they did before. Otherwise, change is temporary, and your people end up reverting to what they were doing before.

I saw transformation in my own company. Once our people clearly understood our core values (who we are), our purpose (why we exist), our vision (where we are going), and our super-objectives (what we want to accomplish every day), my company transformed. It was never the same again. And we achieved extraordinary profits as a result of the transformation.

How did we experience such transformation? Part of the reason was that our leadership team adopted an attitude of serving the people that reported to them (instead of being served by them). As each level of our organization took on this servant leadership approach, we literally turned the traditional pyramid-shaped organizational structure upside down. It began with me at the bottom of the inverted pyramid, serving my direct leadership team. This approach proceeded up the pyramid, level by level, all the way to the top, where our customer contact people were able to respond to and serve our customers. The customer was now at the top of our organizational structure. We'll talk more about this kind of "upside-down leadership" in part 4 as well.

Once our core values, purpose, vision, and super-objectives were clear, we, as leaders, had the responsibility to serve the needs of the employees to help them also accomplish our company's strategies, tactics, and measurable goals through effective leadership.

Servant leadership starts with a vision and ends with a servant heart that helps people live according to that vision.
—KEN BLANCHARD

Your core values, purpose, vision, and super-objectives (e.g., True North Business Essentials) should provide the cornerstone for everything that you do.

Why? Because without them, your organization is like a ship without a rudder and is in danger of drifting aimlessly.

Many organizations lack these essentials, and they tend to jump from task to task without a clear understanding of what bonds the individual actions together and/or the value created by the individual actions.

If you don't give clear direction with your True North Business Essentials, your leadership doesn't matter. Neither does it matter which way you go, because you are lost. One reason organizations become bureaucratic is that no one knows what the organization is supposed to be doing.

> *When you as the leader let your people know what's expected, they can excel.*

Remember the importance of effective leadership. An organization's True North Business Essentials can only be as big as the leader. That is why, as the leader, you must internally champion, consistently live out, and constantly communicate them before you will see outward success.

> *Some men see things as they are and ask why. Others dream things that never were and ask why not.*
> —GEORGE BERNARD SHAW

Take a True North Bearing

What next step can you take right now to discover and share
your WOW!?

The truth is, there was more to our transformation than simply identifying our core values, purpose, vision, and super-objectives. Our secret sauce was how we got there together: through a participative management style where employees were involved in the decision-making process.

Now that you have your roadmap, your compass, your destination, and what you're going to accomplish along the way, it's time to start walking the path that will get you there. And that is the subject of part 4.

PART FOUR

1-2-3

CHAPTER 14

Lone Ranger Leadership Crashes into the Iceberg of Ignorance

Two Traps That Endanger Every Leader

Being a good listener is absolutely critical to being a good leader; you have to listen to the people who are on the front line.
—RICHARD BRANSON

Let's recap where we are on our True North Business journey. You've got your compass (core values and purpose), you know where you're going (your vision), and you know what you want to accomplish every day (your super-objectives). But, as I mentioned in chapter 1, you can have the most accurate compass and most noble destination in the world, but if you don't know the right *path*, you'll never get to where you're going.

Unfortunately, I had to learn this the hard way.

I started working in my father's moving business when I was very young. One of my first jobs was folding the pads used to protect furniture during cross-town (and cross-country) moves. I took pride in the task and tried to fold every pad with excellence. In fact, the moving crews used to call me the "automatic pad folder."

When I was twenty and a recent university graduate, my father unexpectedly died, and I was left with the debt-laden family business, which had five employees and little income.

Although the whole experience was overwhelming, I knew how to run the day-to-day ins and outs of a moving business. And I was confident, like any Texan, that I could "get 'er done!"

Little did I know, but my early years working on the trucks and in the warehouse were my first steps on the path traveled by most entrepreneurs. We start out being doers, the ones involved in actually making a product or providing a service. And in those early stages of business, we are active in every aspect of the business because there is no one else to delegate any work to. This is the Path of Entrepreneurship—taking an idea and mixing in a lot of hard work to create the company that we envision.

Working hard is important, but as your team grows, you realize that being an entrepreneur is not enough. I was beginning to understand there were other paths I had to travel.

The Path of Leadership

As I progressed and matured, I learned more and more about the business. I was also very appreciative of the team around me. Often, I would take time to praise them and speak encouraging words to them. It was common for me to shake their hand or pat them on the back when I encountered them. Like most business owners at this stage, we know we can't do everything alone. Therefore, motivating, encouraging, and guiding those around us becomes very important. We're traveling what I call the Path of Leadership.

At this stage, everything was going pretty well for me. I had always leaned toward leadership, and I had plenty of opportunity to lead in our growing organization. Our company was expanding. People enjoyed working there, and we were successfully profitable. Of course, since there was more to do and more people to lead, I didn't find much time to interact with the people on the front line of our business.

Some days, it seemed like I was on top of the world. Other days, I wanted to beat my head against the wall in my office. More often than not, my problems seemed to stem from people. Why was it so hard to get them to do what I wanted them to do?

Take a True North Bearing

Have you moved from the Path of Entrepreneurship to the Path of Leadership? What new problems did you encounter on the Path of Leadership? Were those problems people-related?

A Wake-Up Call

I guess I would have kept slogging along with our business, doing well but not great. Fortunately, I had a wake-up call. A mentor came into my life who impacted my life and leadership more than any other person. I can still remember the first day that I met him. He exuded confidence, and when our eyes locked, I could see a twinkle in his eye. It was if he knew about a hidden gift and was delighted with the thought of revealing it to those ready to receive it.

The person that I'm referring to is James L. (Jim) Lundy, PhD. Not only was he my coach and mentor for twenty-five years, he was also my friend until the day he died in 2014. When I look back, I now understand that the hidden gift was my potential, and thankfully, over the years, he helped me unwrap it.

Since my own father died, Jim became like a father to me. He would drop anything to help me become a better leader and a better person. I think I tried to implement just about everything he ever suggested, and his recommendations never failed me.

Jim helped me really understand the value of focusing on relationships, so it was my pleasure to invite him to lunch every month or two over his last several years. He taught me so much. He demonstrated what a man of integrity looks like. He was passionate—and I mean passionate—about good customer service. Also, he taught me how to lead people and how to manage the things of the business in a principled way for better results.

In his younger days, he became one of the executives at a small business called The Haloid Company during the years of its most rapid growth. Shortly after he joined Haloid, the name was changed to Xerox. As a consultant, his client list was impressive and included giants such as IBM, 3M, General Mills, TRW, Hewlett-Packard, General Dynamics, and American Express. And then Bobby Albert!

From the moment we met, he persistently kept after me to attend one of his long-running, three-day TRAC 5000 workshops typically held in La Jolla, California.

Sure enough, the first time the TRAC 5000 workshop was held in Wichita Falls, Texas (where Jim chose to make his hometown), I enrolled. For me, the most revealing part of the workshop occurred on the first day, when I read the results from my 360-degree leadership evaluation.

This type of evaluation is based on the anonymous feedback of family, friends, and coworkers. In this case, they had shared their honest thoughts about my leadership. Here's how I'd summarize their main message: "Bobby, when you get an 'idea' for us to carry out, we really want to help you. But get us involved at the *beginning* of your decision-making process and *before* you make a decision about what to do and how to do it."

This unexpected news was stunning. In fact, when I first heard the results, I was mad! It was not until the next morning that I began to cool down and process the findings in a rational way.

To be honest with you, the thoughts that went through my head when I first heard the results from our leadership team were . . .

- They don't understand me.
- They don't understand I was doing them a favor.

- They are busy doing their everyday work, so I'm helping them by not interrupting them to ask their opinion.

For you see, prior to that time, whenever I got an idea for our business, I would come up with *all* of the questions to ask and do *all* the research to determine *all* the answers. I thought this meant I was a good leader.

Then I would go to our leadership team to present my idea and explain how it would work. The team always accepted the ideas, but they would take months and months to roll out. I was constantly having to explain why it was such a good idea. I found myself spending a lot of time and energy pushing and prodding to make it happen. It was draining and discouraging.

Why? Because my employees felt like it was *Bobby's* idea. Since they had no part in the process of developing the idea, they felt no ownership in the final solution or initiative. Also, they were longing for me to ask them for their input. Many times, they had valuable information and unique perspectives on the issue or opportunity at hand.

Take a True North Bearing

Have you ever received honest (even if anonymous) feedback from your team? Do you make decisions and then tell your people what to do?

Two Common Leadership Problems

I was suffering from two common problems that limit the effectiveness of most leaders and keep them from reaching their envisioned future. I just didn't know it.

1. The Path of Lone Ranger Leadership

When it came to making decisions and even setting goals in our organization, I was like the Lone Ranger. After all, wasn't I in charge? This was my first problem.

I would say most leaders follow the Path of Lone Ranger Leadership, where decisions and goals are often imposed from the top of the organization on those below. Yet, with this top-down approach, neither leaders nor employees are very satisfied. Leaders usually find their decisions and goals aren't well implemented while the employees feel decisions and goals are arbitrarily imposed.

2. The Iceberg of Ignorance

The Path of Lone Ranger Leadership (the cause) leads to the second problem (the effect). On my own, I had thought I was doing a good job steering the ship of my business. But, I didn't realize I had actually run aground on an iceberg— the Iceberg of Ignorance.

What is the Iceberg of Ignorance? This principle is popularly attributed to Sidney Yoshida, and I also shared it in *Principled Profits*. It states: "Only 4 percent of an organization's frontline problems are known by top management, 9 percent are known by middle management, 74 percent are known by supervisors, and 100 percent are known by frontline employees."

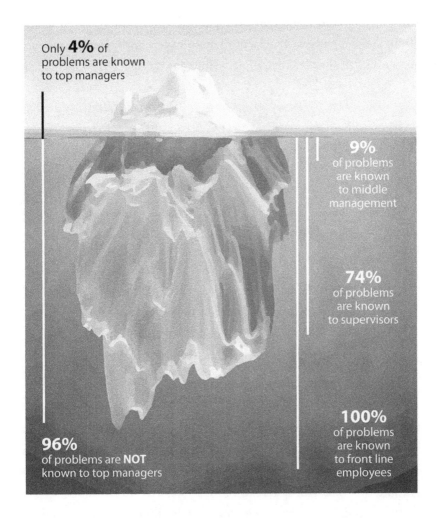

Only **4%** of problems are known to top managers

9% of problems are known to middle management

74% of problems are known to supervisors

100% of problems are known to front line employees

96% of problems are **NOT** known to top managers

Most leaders "don't know what they don't know." Yet, they think they know all of the problems, challenges, and opportunities of their organization. They think that their own skills and expertise are good enough to navigate the waters of business.

This thinking is the strongest among founders or leaders who have been in the organization for many years and are bright and knowledgeable in the technical aspect of their work. However, this ignorance will impede the execution or diminish the results of even the best-laid plans.

Also, they tend to think that their problems and frustrations (a symptom) stem from their employees. That is, until these leaders finally look into the mirror and recognize that they are the problem (the root cause).

The price of greatness is responsibility.
—WINSTON CHURCHILL

Take a True North Bearing

Do you think it's possible that your lack of connection with your frontline people has limited the effectiveness of your leadership? Have you considered there might be problems residing below the surface of your reality?

On the first day of that workshop, the 360-degree evaluation forced me to look in the mirror: as a leader, I really did not seek, listen to, and learn from my people's insights and advice. The Path of Lone Ranger Leadership had run me straight into the Iceberg of Ignorance.

In other words, using the terminology of John Maxwell, I was the lid on our company's success.

Fortunately, this realization also helped me move from the commonly traveled Path of Lone Ranger Leadership to the lightly traveled, but very rewarding, Path of Effective Leadership—the fifth True North Business essential we discussed in part 1.

Take a True North Bearing

Are you a Lone Ranger when making decisions and setting goals? How has that approach impacted the effectiveness of your team?

The Motivation Survey

Based on Yoshida's statistics, it's likely that you, too, have "cold feet," standing on top of your own iceberg. For me, it took a shocking 360-degree evaluation to wake me up and reveal a better way to lead. But, you don't have to attend years of the school of hard knocks like I did to learn the better way to lead your organization.

I've discovered an easier way to reach the Path of Effective Leadership. It starts with a simple survey about motivation. Don't be alarmed! This is a survey, not a test. Your answers should reflect your beliefs and feelings—and they can't be judged as right or wrong. How you feel is how you feel.

So, here is the survey. Consider downloading this Motivation Survey so that you can print it and easily record your own answers. Navigate to TNB-book.com to download the survey.

As you read each statement, you might want to mark it with a Y for yes, agree, or probably true or an N for no, disagree, or unlikely.

____ 1. I would rather be living in 1850, and I wish that I were an indentured servant.

____ 2. I enjoy achieving goals and receiving recognition for my achievements.

____ 3. I would rather be asked to do something instead of being ordered to do it.

___ 4. I enjoy having someone ask me for my opinion or advice, and I feel good when others listen to me. I also appreciate not being interrupted.

___ 5. I can get frustrated trying to explain something to someone who has already made up his mind and who won't even try to understand the additional information or point of view I am presenting.

___ 6. I am likely to feel better (more interested, less frustrated, etc.) if I have at least some input and influence about matters concerning me.

___ 7. Time goes faster for me when I am busy, and I tend to get turned on by a sense of achievement or recognition for achievement.

___ 8. I would prefer to have 10 percent more income even if, to receive it, I had to work on a different job where the work was of no apparent value or importance.

___ 9. When I make a mistake, it helps me become more motivated and effective if people point out how stupid or ineffective I am—particularly in front of others.

___ 10. If I ask my subordinates for their ideas or advice, they most certainly will think I am weak and, as a consequence, respect me less as a manager.

The Answers

I have found that this survey is a powerful tool to help you think more deeply about this important topic of motivation. Let's take a look at your answers to these questions and see what we can learn about motivation:

1. I would rather be living in 1850, and I wish that I were an indentured servant.

I've never had anyone answer yes to this statement. The fact is, people who have spread their wings personally and professionally want to feel useful intellectually as well as physically. Certainly being "just a servant" isn't appealing to them.

2. I enjoy achieving goals and receiving recognition for my achievements.

Virtually everybody agrees with this. That's why they play golf, why Little Leaguers want to get base hits, and why kids smile proudly when they've aced a test.

3. I would rather be asked to do something instead of being ordered to do it.

Sure. Most people feel better when they are treated considerately. And, of course, when ordered to do something, we feel more like a servant, and we're back into the situation presented in statement number one.

4. I enjoy having someone ask me for my opinion or advice, and I feel good when others listen to me. I also appreciate not being interrupted.

Most of us enjoy being considered worthy of having potentially useful opinions. When we're interrupted, the other person is demonstrating that our opinions aren't very worthwhile.

It's easy to conclude that if our opinions aren't worthwhile then we, as individuals, aren't worthwhile—and that certainly doesn't help us feel good about ourselves.

5. I can get frustrated trying to explain something to someone who has already made up his mind and who won't even try to understand the additional information or point of view I am presenting.

This is what happens when we're talking with someone who already has made up his mind—as is the case when something has already been decided and the advocate is hoping to get buy-in. In these situations, we feel as if we're talking to a brick wall, and who among us would be happy wasting time that way?

So, most people agree with this statement. However, we should note that some people have pointed out that even though we may not feel good about being ignored, we should be mature enough that we would not allow ourselves to become frustrated over it. So, they answer no.

6. I am likely to feel better (more interested, less frustrated, etc.) if I have at least some input and influence about matters concerning me.

Most people answer yes to this one. For example, most janitors would appreciate being asked about what brand of buffing compound they'd like to use.

If an aloof purchasing agent buys the compound without asking the janitor about it, the agent can be viewed as considering the janitor to be *just* a janitor—and nobody wants to be seen as *just* anything.

7. Time goes faster for me when I am busy, and I tend to get turned on by a sense of achievement or recognition for achievement.

Isn't it interesting how some days seem to just fly by? All of a sudden, we may realize it's time to go home. And, boy, doesn't it feel good to have accomplished all that we did?

8. I would prefer to have 10 percent more income even if, to receive it, I had to work on a different job where the work was of no apparent value or importance.

Think about this. Most people recognize that there's no way they'd be willing to push against a brick wall fifty-five minutes per hour for eight hours a day, day after day. There'd be no way to gain a sense of achievement and worthiness.

9. When I make a mistake, it helps me become more motivated and effective if people point out how stupid or ineffective I am—particularly in front of others.

I don't know of anyone who would agree with this statement. There's a long-standing recommendation about praising in public and criticizing in private. We've never run across anyone who revels in being publicly criticized or demeaned.

Also, it's been suggested that corrective advice be phrased along the lines of looking forward to opportunity rather than backward to blame.

For example, "You're still messing up on 4 percent of these" doesn't help me maintain or enhance my sense of self-worth. "Is there some way we could achieve a higher success rate than 96 percent?" presents a challenge without making me feel inadequate.

10. If I ask my subordinates for their ideas or advice, they most certainly will think I am weak and, as a consequence, respect me less as a manager.

Most people admit that this is an unreasonable statement. First, no supervisor is expected to know everything—and shouldn't pretend he or she does.

Second, almost all subordinates can contribute useful insights and suggestions when they are asked, and they enjoy being respected as worthy participants in decision-making processes. And, as a friend once pointed out, "You can't have an inspired set of associates if you ask them to check their brains at the door!"

The Final Question

In my conversations with supervisors, managers, and executives of organizations throughout the country, they often ask about employee motivation. Their questions are typically along the lines of, "What should I do *to* my people to make them have my sense of responsibility, dependability, and excitement about providing our customers with value-adding products and services that exceed their expectations?"

That's an interesting question. And an important one. Think about it: Are the people who work for you human? Do they have feelings? Do you suppose they, too, want to feel good about themselves? Do they (or would they) like to be dealt with in ways that will help them maintain or enhance their feelings of self-worth? You can bet on it!

Let's go back to the question: "What should I do *to* my people to make them . . .?" The answer, of course, is not to do anything *to* them but to start doing more things *with* them!

The eleventh question wasn't included as part of the original Motivation Survey, but, in a sense, it may be the most important question of this exercise. Can you guess the final question that ties this whole process into a powerful experience?

Here's the question: "How do you suppose the people who work for you would answer this Motivation Survey?"

When I bring up this question in workshops, there's usually a moment of absolute silence. Eventually, someone quietly ventures out by whispering, "The same?" Of course!

Take a True North Bearing

Do you like achieving goals and receiving recognition for achievement? Do you like being asked for your opinion and advice? When someone orders you to do a task, how does that make you feel?

As a True North Business leader, which would you rather have: employees who are content doing the bare minimum each day or a team with fire in the belly to achieve great things with you?

Do you want to learn what is really going on with your frontline people as they serve your customers and interact with your suppliers? Do you want to run your business more efficiently and effectively? Do you want to deliver the highest-quality products and services on time, every time, in a way that is the most convenient for your customers? Do you want your employees to come to work excited every day about what they will accomplish? Do you want to make extraordinary profits way beyond your wildest dreams?

Of course! Right? Well . . .

I finally came to my senses and accepted the horrible truth—most of my *outside* challenges were because of *inside* problems. I discovered if I wanted to have a significant impact on the growth of our company, I needed to change how I led our people.

In the next chapter, I'd like to introduce a new approach to leading your people, one that will allow you to effectively melt the Iceberg of Ignorance and follow the Path of Effective Leadership.

CHAPTER 15

A New Way to Lead

Change Your Leadership, Change Your Results

When leaders throughout an organization take an active, genuine interest in the people they manage, when they invest real time to understand employees at a fundamental level, they create a climate for greater morale, loyalty, and, yes, growth.
—PATRICK LENCIONI

"You won't believe what they did to us at work today!" I'm sure that you have heard this comment before. You may have even said it yourself.

One day, an executive I'm mentoring excitedly told me how he came up with a great, new quality improvement process to better manage his company's inventory. Based on his own knowledge and experience, and with the best of intentions, he wrote out the new quality improvement policy and its new procedures without input from any of his employees. Then he presented the new policy and procedures to the manager and the frontline employees.

What happened next, you most likely already know. The new policy and procedures did get implemented but with very little enthusiasm. You probably also know the rest of the story: under each employee's breath, there was a silent pushback. And when these employees went home that night, over dinner with their spouse or a friend, they most likely said, "You won't believe what they did to us at work today!"

In the case of my executive client, if his employees had been asked for their input, which they would have gladly given, they could have helped the executive write even better policy and procedures. And they would have done so with great enthusiasm.

I've discovered that poor decision making can sap the enthusiasm of your people and create poor results for your entire organization.

Take a True North Bearing

Have you ever tried to lead a group of people, but the people did not want to follow? Did it seem like they didn't see the benefits of getting on board with your goals and direction?

How to Lose Your Best Employees

Imagine this scenario: you arrive at work one day to discover your workstation has been moved. You didn't know it was going to happen, and you don't know why it happened. Then you learn that your senior manager decided she wanted to rearrange the seating so it would be easier for her to remember your names or your faces and where you sat.

This is exactly what happened to a client I was consulting with, and the employees of that department were pretty upset with their manager. How do you think you would feel if this seating change happened to you?

- *Unsettled and upset?* There is a certain element of security in the constancy of how we arrange our workspaces and knowing who our neighbors are.

- *Unappreciated and undervalued?* Unilateral decisions made without the input of those affected almost always devalue the people involved.
- *Angry and resentful?* After an invasion of your privacy or your space, you are not likely to recommend your workplace as a wonderful place to be.

As we discussed in chapter 2, effective leaders focus on both enhancing relationships *and* driving for results, not merely one or the other. They also make decisions based on principles, rather than expediency. If we can get past the scarcity mindset that leads to expedient, dictatorial leadership, we can enjoy the abundance that results from selfless, others-focused leadership.

Yet, it's common for leaders to focus on results and disregard the relationship side of their work. Why do leaders drive for results at the expense of relationships?

Unfortunately, as leaders are promoted into higher levels in their organization, too many feel that they should become more dynamic and decisive. After all, they're in charge. And the more dynamic and decisive they become, the more likely they are to disregard maintaining and enhancing relationships as they expediently focus on their drive for results. Isn't that all that matters?

The fact is, the more relationship-conscious employees are, the quicker they become disenchanted with leaders who rule with selfish expediency, pursuing individual and departmental goals that are self-focused without considering the rest of the team.

Employees want to be respected and invited to use their minds instead of just blindly following orders. They can quickly become disenchanted with supervisors who express, "My way or the highway!" or "Do it because I said to!" or "Do it because I'm the boss!"

What happens next is predictable—and avoidable. The good employees quit because they feel undervalued. The mediocre employees stay because they're content with a paycheck and with being told what to do. If the manager never changes, when new employees are hired, it isn't long before the cycle begins again. This shortsighted approach will never produce top-notch teams.

Insanity is doing the same thing, over and over again,
but expecting different results.
—ANONYMOUS

Take a True North Bearing

What are you doing to motivate your employees so they don't
say, "You won't believe what they did to us at work today"?

The Secret to Employee Motivation

The key to motivation is *engagement*. Gallup's 2016 State of the American Workplace report stated that only three in ten employees strongly agree that at work their opinions seem to count. Gallup also reported, "By moving that ratio to 6 in 10 employees, organizations could realize a 27 percent reduction in turnover, a 40 percent reduction in safety incidents, and a 12 percent increase in productivity."[17]

Extensive research compiled in Gallup's 2016 report also reveals that employees fall into one of three groups:

- *33 percent engaged*: "Employees are highly involved in and enthusiastic about their work and workplace. They are psychological 'owners,' drive performance and innovation, and move the organization forward."[18]
- *51 percent not engaged*: "Employees are psychologically unattached to their work and company. Because their engagement needs are not being

---

17   Gallup, "State of the American Workplace 2016," p. 112, available at https://news.gallup.com/reports/199961/7.aspx.
18   Gallup, "State of the American Workplace 2016," p. 63.

fully met, they're putting time—but not energy or passion—into their work."[19]

- *16 percent actively disengaged*: "Employees aren't just unhappy at work—they are resentful that their needs aren't being met and are acting out their unhappiness. Every day, these workers potentially undermine what their engaged coworkers accomplish."[20]

What difference does employee engagement make? Well, here's a practical example. Whenever a company offers a promotion, wage increase, or bonus to their employees, the type of company the employees work for will determine their perspective on what they have received. Let's look at two different companies.

Company A seeks to actively engage their employees. This company . . .

- Understands that they need to pay their people a fair wage and engage their employees.
- Has built a culture where people thrive, and profits are soaring.
- Has a leadership team who truly knows why their people are happy and their bottom line is increasing.

This means its employees . . .

- Go to work feeling enthusiastic, excited, and passionate because their employer understands the importance of enhancing relationships as they drive for results.
- Accept promotions, wage increases, and bonuses with an attitude of gratitude and with a grateful heart.

Company B does *not* focus on engaging their employees, leaving many of their employees feeling disengaged or actively disengaged. This company . . .

19 Gallup, "State of the American Workplace 2016," p. 63.
20 Gallup, "State of the American Workplace 2016," p. 63.

- Thinks that if they only pay their people more money than the competition, their employees will work harder and deliver more results.
- Has built a culture where people are giving up, and profits are either stagnant or declining.
- Has a management team who cannot figure out why their people are not delivering better results since they are paying them more to do so.

This means its employees . . .

- Go to work feeling their work is like "pushing rope" or "pressing their hand hard against the wall" for eight long hours because their boss is only driving for results.
- Accept promotions, wage increases, and bonuses with an attitude of entitlement because they feel that they deserve the extra benefits.
- Can you see how engagement leads to motivation?

Money buys movement, not motivation.

As you saw in the scenario of Company A, when you pay your people a fair wage and engage your employees, you will gain the results you have searched for.

Take a True North Bearing

Which leader would you want to work for—
Company A's or Company B's?
Which perspective do your employees have when
you give them extra pay or benefits?

What Employees Really Want

I believe all leaders—whether a CEO, president, owner, or leader of a division, department, or function—would agree that if they met the expressed needs of a potential external customer, that customer would be willing to buy the company's products and/or services.

However, most leaders do not understand the felt needs of their *internal* customers. Their internal customers are their employees. Interestingly, it is only through the hard work and help of their internal customers (employees) that leaders can achieve the results they desire.

Take a True North Bearing

Are you totally satisfied with your results as a leader? Would you consider changing your approach in order to produce better results?

With 67 percent of employees either not engaged or actively disengaged, these findings from Gallup are rather sobering. But, every problem creates the opportunity for a solution. And I see this as a huge opportunity to improve the American workplace by addressing the problems and creating cultures where people thrive and profits soar and where all leaders can effectively lead their team toward its True North.

So, what are the felt needs of employees (internal customers)? Most employees want the leaders of their organization to

- Demonstrate that they care for them as an individual.
- Understand that they can and want to contribute toward the organization's goals.
- Provide a culture where they have a sense of belonging.

- Create an environment of constant learning so they feel they can do their best.
- Stand for something that they feel good about—something they can support.

Why, then, is there such a gap between what leaders want and what employees want? Is it possible that the leader is the one who is disengaged or actively disengaged? Is it time for the leader to take a good, long look at herself in the mirror? Is it possible the reason the CEOs (and the leaders of a division or department) are not having the results they so much desire is because they are the lid on their organization's successful results?

Take a True North Bearing

Are there limits to your leadership lid? Are you open to changing your leadership style?

A Participative Leadership Style

Back to my wake-up call at the three-day leadership conference, where I had just realized that I was the lid on my company's success. As the conference progressed, Jim Lundy encouraged the attendees to maintain and enhance relationships as we drove for results. As you may remember from part 1, this kind of leadership style is also part of the Path of Effective Leadership.

Most managers, while intelligent and well-meaning, tend to expediently "prepare the path" to drive for results. They tell their subordinates the results (the what) they want, with little or no input (the how) from their subordinates. These managers don't realize that investing in relationships actually helps achieve significantly better results.

This relationship-oriented, participative leadership style prepares the employees for the twists and turns along the path as they serve customers, suppliers (yes, even suppliers), and each other. Employees who feel valued are much more willing to go the extra mile when those twists and turns happen—and they always happen.

An employee's sense of ownership over a product or process translates into positive results:

- Better customer service
- Better accuracy
- Better attitude overall
- A more positive workplace, even during seasons of stress

Treat an employee like a robot, however, and watch production and satisfaction plummet. Instead of taking ownership and trying to solve problems, employees, feeling overwhelmed and disregarded, will shift blame and responsibilities to others.

Here lies the paradox. Most leaders assume that strong leadership means independent action and that greater control produces greater results. However, and ironically, the reverse is true.

The Participatory Paradox: The more leaders include others in the decision-making process, the stronger the results and leadership. Likewise, the more leaders exert absolute control, the weaker the results and leadership.

When I got back to work, I began to incorporate a more participative leadership style. One of the most powerful changes I made was how I made decisions that would broadly impact an area, department, or the entire company.

I started to actively seek the opinion and input of others at the beginning of the decision-making process and before I made a decision. I call this approach *Engage2Lead.*

Engage2Lead involves asking for and considering employees' input when making decisions, which leads to better and more informed decision-making results.

The results were transformational. I made better decisions, *and* we created a team that naturally felt a sense of ownership and responsibility for their contributions.

Does It Have to Be Lonely at the Top?

Until you have experienced it yourself, it may be hard to understand the oft-repeated phrase, "It's lonely at the top." But, when you are the leader of an organization, department, or even a small group, you realize how true that statement is. As CEO of our company, I knew this feeling all too well—until I changed my approach to leadership.

Alone we can do so little; together we can do so much.
—HELEN KELLER

I have also observed that the days of leaders having to "know it all" are quickly vanishing as organizations face unprecedented change, competition, and stagnant organic growth. Leaders cannot survive on their own, nor do they have *all* the answers.

Take a True North Bearing

Have you been a Lone Ranger leader like I was? Are you tired of trying to know it all? Have you considered that better decision making leads to better results?

There is a better way. A way that provides a lifeline of hope for the isolated, drowning leader. It involves asking for and considering employees' input, which leads to more informed and better decision-making results.

I don't know about you, but after I had my wake-up call, I knew I needed other people to help me get the job done.

My loneliness started to fade away as I began to adopt the Engage2Lead approach to making decisions. And more importantly, my team became more motivated and engaged than ever before.

I know, you're thinking, "That's easier said than done!" In the next chapter, I'm going to share an easy way to get on the Path of Effective Leadership and involve your team in your decisions for the best results *and* relationships.

CHAPTER 16

It's as Easy as 1-2-3

Improve Your Outcomes with This
Participative Leadership Approach

All employees have an innate desire to contribute
to something bigger than themselves.
—JAG RANDHAWA

Not long ago, I read about a survey of workers in the United States who were asked if they could work harder on the job than they currently were. Of those surveyed, 85 percent said that they could. And more than half claimed that they could double their effectiveness "if I wanted to." I don't know about you, but I want the people I lead to "want to" be as effective as they possibly can *all* the time.

We would rather have one man or woman working
with us than three merely working for us.
—F. W. WOOLWORTH

A key to motivating folks is to start doing things *with* your people, not doing things *to* your people. And one way of doing more things with your people is by including them in your decision-making process through the participative leadership approach I call Engage2Lead.

And one of the best ways for you to take the first step toward participative leadership is through the 1-2-3 leadership practice.

1-2-3 is a unique approach leaders can use to facilitate the decision-making process. At the very *beginning* of the decision-making process—and *before* making a decision—the empowering leader seeks input from his employees. Such a leader asks these three questions:

1. Who can help me make a better decision?
2. Who will have to carry it out?
3. Who will be impacted by it?

The answers to the three questions will guide you to assemble the right people and involve them as appropriate to help make important decisions.

When you, as the leader, involve the right people in your decision making, your team will have a better understanding of and commitment to the decision *you* collaboratively set. And they take pride in the achievement of decisions when they are involved in the development, creation, and implementation stages. When employees provide the necessary input, how can they complain about implementing their own plans?

And as the leader, you can avoid employees who:

- Lack a feeling of ownership or commitment
- Drag their heels in implementation
- Resort to sabotaging the plans

Now that you understand how the 1-2-3 practice can transform decision making, let me tell you what it's not:

1. It does not mean running your organization as a democracy. This is not decision making by committee. As the leader, you always have ultimate

authority and responsibility for decisions and results, and you must still decide the future direction for the organization.

This is not decision making by committee.

2. It does not mean creating consensus decisions among all members of your team. Consensus decisions usually take forever to be reached and yield diluted results.
3. It is not always the right decision-making approach. We'll discuss this point in detail later in this chapter. But, although there may be times this process-oriented strategy isn't best, it's generally the most powerful approach a leader can take when driving for results—which is why it's the best path for pursuing your envisioned future in your organization.

Take a True North Bearing

Do you make a decision and then dictate the operating instructions to your followers? Or do you engage your people at the beginning of the decision-making process?

How Does 1-2-3 Work?

The 1-2-3 practice is a helpful technique for decision making. For this tool to work best, it requires discipline at several stages:

1. *Use 1-2-3 frequently.* Its use should be a way of life. You miss out on so much of the power of this process if you only employ it when it's convenient or when you happen to think about it.

2. *Use 1-2-3 before you come up with your own preliminary solutions.* As soon as the need for a decision is recognized, the 1-2-3 questions can be addressed. If not, the initiator will tend to start making preliminary judgments that she may feel compelled to defend when the decision-exploring team convenes.

> *I've learned not to write down any preliminary thoughts before a group meets so that I keep an open mind to others' ideas.*
> —Bobby Albert

Once you answer the three questions and know who to include in your decision, how do you get their input? Instead of meeting individually (a key mistake) with those who come to mind when answering the 1-2-3 questions, meet with them as a group and have an open discussion of the pros and cons of the matter in question.

Please note that after all of the pros and cons have been considered, the initiator still has to make the final decision. Again, the 1-2-3 process is not decision by a committee.

If a decision is relatively straightforward, one group meeting for input may be enough. However, when a change, idea, opportunity, or problem facing you is big, it is best to engage your team over a period of time through a series of meetings.

A good four-step approach is to

1. Start with a meeting to expose your team to the change, idea, opportunity, or problem and then give them some time to let the information incubate.
2. Pull them together again and ask for and record their input about things to consider and what suggested decision to make.
3. Frame a decision and meet with your team to review, tweak, and create buy-in for the decision.
4. Have the team review the final decision to see if there are any more ideas for improving it.

And don't forget to include customers and suppliers in the 1-2-3 process when it makes sense. Many times, their input and feedback are important as you consider adding new services or goods to your product mix, making changes in your operating schedules, or changing how your organization provides services.

Give me a fish and I eat for a day.
Teach me to fish and I eat for a lifetime.
—CHINESE PROVERB

Take a True North Bearing

How do you make decisions? Do you make decisions alone? What process does your organization use to promote teamwork when facing challenges, considering opportunities, making decisions, or setting goals?

After you use the 1-2-3 practice to engage your employees and receive their input—whether you held one group meeting or several—you are ready for the three final steps in your decision-making process.

1. Make the final decision.

Now it's time for you to make the decision. Yes, *you* still must decide.

I asked, "Why doesn't somebody do something?" Then I
realized I was somebody.
—UNKNOWN

Making the final decision is your right and responsibility as a leader and just another step in the 1-2-3 process. But now, your decision making is informed by the research and recommendations of your team members. The end results will be a good decision and a supportive and aligned team.

A real decision is measured by the fact that you've taken a new action. If there's no action, you haven't truly decided.
—TONY ROBBINS

2. Provide timely feedback.

Giving your people feedback on the what and the why of a decision is critical, especially if it goes against some of the information, advice, and/or recommendations they provided. It keeps them involved in the process and committed to the results. And it helps your people to feel that their involvement and thoughts shared did not go into a black hole.

It also gives you a chance to recognize and thank them for their contributions during the process and to solicit their help in implementing the decision. After all, the job isn't done when your decision is made. The decision still needs to be implemented, and your team must remain committed to ensure smooth implementation.

3. Manage the change.

Using the 1-2-3 practice to structure the decision-making process will equip you to make the best possible decision. Providing your team with feedback prepares them to implement the decision you have chosen in an efficient and effective way.

To manage the change and the implementation of the decision, you can continue the 1-2-3 process through regular exchanges with team members and reviews of progress (intermediate milestones).

Take a True North Bearing

How might 1-2-3 help you make better decisions and ease implementation of decisions you make so your people will "want to"? How well do you give your people feedback once you make a decision?

Who Should Use 1-2-3?

A 1-2-3 approach to decision making is not something that is reserved only for top or middle managers or supervisors. It is a process that can and should be used by everyone in an organization, from the person in the corner office to the people on the front line, as situations call for it.

When Should 1-2-3 Be Used?

When 1-2-3 should be used is a trickier question. A 1-2-3 approach obviously isn't necessary for routine decisions required in the course of day-to-day business. Nor is it a good approach when following a set procedure, regardless of what kind of business you are involved in.

In general, the more significant a decision is or the broader its impact, the more it calls for the 1-2-3 practice to structure the process.

But, sometimes, even the most significant decisions do not lend themselves to a 1-2-3 approach for any number of reasons. For example, if the owner of a company is considering selling the business or if he is considering an offer to buy another company, those discussions of a possible sale or purchase must be limited.

In fact, in these types of situations, nondisclosure or confidentiality agreements usually will restrict the disclosure of information to people with a "need to know" because of the sensitive nature of the subjects and the risks of the information being made public prematurely.

Progress with 1-2-3

Even though using 1-2-3 takes longer on the front-end than other ways of making decisions, it saves you as much (or more) time on the back-end. In fact, 1-2-3 facilitates progress for two simple reasons:

1. You have made a reasoned decision based on more and better information than you would have collected on your own; and
2. The process keeps your people moving forward instead of having to backtrack or go sideways because of decisions reached without their commitment and support.

> *Build with your team a feeling of oneness, of dependence on one another, and of strength derived from unity in the pursuit of your objective.*
> —VINCE LOMBARDI

Take a True North Bearing

What important decision can you make today using the 1-2-3 decision-making process? After you lead your people through your first 1-2-3 guided decision, including follow-up, how would you rate the quality of the decision? How about the engagement of your team?

As you can see, it's important for you as a leader to fully tap the power of the 1-2-3 leadership practice by making the final decision, providing feedback to your team, and managing the change created by your decision. When you do, you'll be well on your way to doubling the effectiveness of your team by motivating your team to "want to," and to "give it their all."

CHAPTER 17

1-2-3 in Action

*Empower Your Teams at Work, at Home,
and Even with Volunteers*

*Show me an organization in which employees take ownership, and I
will show you one that beats its competitors.*
—MICHAEL ABRASHOFF

So, what do the Engage2Lead approach and the 1-2-3 practice look like in action?

1-2-3 at Work

With good up-front coordination, adopting a participative Engage2Lead decision-making approach, with the 1-2-3 practice underpinning your efforts, can guide teams to discover ideas that far exceed any one leader's expectations or abilities. And that's exactly what happened when we invited the participation of all our people to help make the decisions associated with a big opportunity that presented its share of obstacles.

Years ago, I seized an opportunity to grow our operations in a big way. First, I rolled out the good news to our leadership team. My voice and verbal pace quickened (as much as possible for a Texas boy) as I shared my exciting news with them: "We've just purchased eight acres, including some existing facilities, that we'll transform into our new offices!" After some positive feedback and some clarifying Q&A, they soon began to think about the associated "bad news."

This also meant that we would be consolidating our current nine (yes, nine) different office and warehouse facilities into the new location. The leadership and logistical challenges seemed overwhelming, but it proved to be an opportunity for significant growth, unity, and teamwork.

> *Teamwork is the ability to work together toward a common vision. . . . It is the fuel that allows common people to attain uncommon results.*
> —ANDREW CARNEGIE

If you've been in leadership very long, you know that big moves mean big changes, and big changes are opportunities to grow—but change also comes with significant leadership challenges. Dealing with change can be difficult. It's human nature to get comfortable with the status quo. We all like the familiarity that comes with routine.

We knew that the impending move was going to require a lot of change, and to do it right, we needed a lot of buy-in and help from everyone in our organization. When faced with such a challenge, what's a leader to do? Well, I'm sure we didn't do things perfectly, but we used a unique approach to handle the big move and inspire our people in the process.

Earlier in my leadership development, I would have dived into this massive project headfirst. After days of thinking and planning and creating long to-do lists, I would have called my leadership team together for the big reveal. Then I would've shared the news of the big project, along with my plans for how we would tackle the many associated challenges.

Fortunately, for the big consolidation move, I chose a different approach. I embraced the Engage2Lead participative leadership approach and leveraged the 1-2-3 practice. At the very beginning of the decision-making process—and before making a decision—I asked myself these questions:

1. Who can help me make a better decision?
2. Who will have to carry it out?
3. Who will be impacted by it?

In considering these 1-2-3 questions, I realized that I needed to involve the whole company with the decision-making process related to the move. So, I chose to shut the entire company down for a half-day training to focus on the following questions:

- What would be good characteristics/behaviors/attitudes of our service toward our external customers at our new location?
- What barriers or challenges will there be for us at the new location?
- What have we done particularly well or not so well regarding internal customer teamwork?
- What specific steps (regarding actions, behaviors, and attitudes) should we take as individuals and teams to maximize the effectiveness of our company as we look toward future growth?

Wow! We received a boatload of amazing feedback and great suggestions from our people, and they also became really excited about helping us move to the new facilities.

Take a True North Bearing

For what upcoming important decision can you use the 1-2-3 practice to guide your decision-making process? Which one of the four questions above would help you achieve the greatest ideas and suggestions?

Why should you try these new methods in your business? I believe the leadership approach of Engage2Lead and the questions of the 1-2-3 practice help create an energized and efficient team.

1. An energized team

When a leader engages his people in the decision-making process, several positive results are set into motion.

Team members who are involved in the process become more and more enthusiastic and energized about it as they go along. It allows the leader to show that he values his people's abilities as well as their knowledge. This builds trust between the leader and his team. The team's desire for the success of the process (and the result) grows. Team members' enthusiasm also grows and becomes contagious, lifting the team to higher performance. An energized team will overcome obstacles and cheer on the new project at critical points along the way.

2. An efficient team

As you engage your team by asking them to participate in the decision-making process, they learn more about the key issues. And they take more ownership and become excited about the challenges and opportunities being considered. Educated, vested, and energized teams implement decisions with enthusiasm and purpose. Plus, there is little time spent selling them on the decision because they have already bought into it.

And, their knowledge and ownership of the project and their energy propel them to implement a decision with excellence. An informed team also experiences fewer surprises as they roll out new initiatives.

With good up-front coordination, adopting a participative Engage2Lead leadership style that employs 1-2-3 questions can guide teams to discover ideas that far exceed any one leader's expectations or abilities. And that's exactly what happened when we invited the participation of all our people to help make the decisions associated with our big move.

Take a True North Bearing

Do you see how employing the Engage2Lead leadership approach can help you make better decisions and confront changes facing your organization?

1-2-3 at Home

Leading a family resembles leading a team in the workplace, which means the 1-2-3 practice is just as useful at home as at work. Before I share with you how we used 1-2-3 in our parenting, I want to explain a little bit about the context.

To lead our "home team," my wife and I made specific decisions about how we would teach and guide our boys. For example, instead of creating a *Better Homes and Gardens* house, when our three boys were young, we converted our formal living room and connecting dining room into an entertainment area for them and their friends.

It included a nice-size pool table and a TV area supplied with pre-selected movie videos and video games. We also kept the pantry and refrigerator well stocked for them and their friends.

When weather permitted, they could also go outside in the backyard to our swimming pool and/or play basketball. Also, the kids seemed to think my charcoal-grilled hamburgers were the world's greatest (my secret was fresh meat marinated in smoke sauce).

As you can imagine, our home was a real gathering place for a bunch of good kids. Our boys were always inviting their friends to come over to our home because it was a safe place without parents hovering over their every move.

And that is actually why my wife and I invested our time and resources in this way—so we could get to know who our boys' friends were and who they chose to hang out with.

Our boys clearly knew the boundary lines of our "House Rules" (e.g., no R-rated movies), but they also knew they had age-appropriate freedoms within those boundary lines. Their friends, as well, knew our House Rules, communicated not by my wife and me but by our boys.

You may be wondering why I'm telling you about all of this. To be clear, I will be the first to share that my wife and I are definitely not perfect parents. We made a lot of mistakes, but we chose to also live by those same House Rules to set an example for our boys. And this story has truths that reach beyond the home and into the workplace.

I'm fully convinced that since our boys clearly understood the boundary lines of our House Rules and had the freedom to be involved to make decisions and choices between those boundary lines, they reaped several benefits, such as:

- Learning that when they made principled and wise decisions, there were blessings, success, and growth, but when they made wrong and expedient decisions, there were negative consequences
- Understanding that with their freedoms came responsibilities

Adopting the House Rules as their own resulted in them enforcing the rules with their friends. They have continued, even to this day, to live out those House Rules, maturing into honorable men who have wonderful wives (who are like daughters to my wife and me) and excellent jobs. They manage their money well, are involved in their church, and are better dads than I was. I'm so proud of them!

Prepare the child for the path,
not the path for the child.
—Betsy Brown Braun

All too often, this philosophy plays out backward with well-meaning parents who believe their task is primarily to prepare the path for their children. These parents remove obstacles, smooth out the rough places, and generally make life a painless, trouble-free experience. However, what happens on the inside (how the child is maturing) will have far more influence on the child's future life than the external things that tend to consume the parents' energy and emotions.

Take a True North Bearing

Are you preparing your children for the path or the path for your children? What steps can you take today to adopt this approach and start earning the enthusiasm, initiative, and devotion of your family?

With the boundaries clear, we could give our kids plenty of freedom within those boundaries, such as including them in important decisions. And that's where 1-2-3 comes in. Good things happened when we asked our two older sons, who had already married, and our youngest son, who was near finishing college, to help plan a holiday vacation. Specifically, we asked them to get involved in the decision-making process to find a common place where everyone could meet for a family vacation during Thanksgiving.

During this process, I was amazed how . . .

- Everyone became so excited and interested in the vacation as the process went forward.
- These Internet-savvy boys and the two older boys' wives jumped in with both feet and researched travel options online with ease.
- They interacted well to make recommendations for my wife and me to consider as we made the final decision.

This decision-making process worked so well, I wish I had started this process sooner when our boys were younger.

Summer is the time for family trips and outings, but figuring out a plan that suits everyone can be tricky. Giving children a voice and having them take part in a family decision-making process can teach them very valuable leadership skills that they someday will also take into the workplace as adults.

As we *engaged* in this decision-making process, we all learned to . . .

- Advocate for what we wanted
- Listen to others' wishes
- Make compromises
- Accept being exposed to something new

Today, at the very beginning of your decision-making process for your family's summer vacation—and before making a decision—seek to engage your children for the best summer vacation your family will ever have. I've created a Family Vacation Discussion Guide with tips and suggested questions to help guide your family discussion. You can download it at TNB-book.com.

Take a True North Bearing

Have you ever engaged your children in the family vacation decision-making process? What were the results?

1-2-3 in Volunteer Leadership

Many years ago, I was asked to be the president of my local Rotary Club, an international volunteer service organization. A few weeks before I started, I asked our board of directors if it would be okay for me to arrange an off-site club assembly at the home of one of our members. As you can imagine, serving delicious charcoal-grilled hamburgers resulted in almost 100 percent attendance, along with lots of fellowship.

Then I did something that never had been done in our club before (at that point, I hadn't done it in our business, either). I invited people to choose one of the four main planning groups. And, in advance, I asked key leaders of each group to facilitate discussions on one of four main subjects and record the input from everyone who participated.

It was amazing how enthusiastic people were coming out of those discussion groups. Although I didn't use the 1-2-3 questions in particular in this case, I understand now that the participative decision-making process we went through was the secret to our successful follow-through during my year as Rotary Club president. It wasn't too long after my year ended that I was asked to serve at the next level as the Rotary International district governor and was the youngest in the world at that time.

Volunteers will certainly test your leadership skills to the maximum, but a participative decision-making approach is the key to effectively leading anyone, even volunteers.

Take a True North Bearing

Have you had the opportunity to lead volunteers? What challenges and frustrations came along with your leadership role? How might your results change if you start using the 1-2-3 practice to guide decision making with your volunteers?

We've discussed the what, how, who, when, and where (through case studies) of 1-2-3. But, the most important question is, why? In the next chapter, we'll look at the benefits of using 1-2-3 for you and your organization.

CHAPTER 18

The Benefits of 1-2-3

Enjoy More Engaged,
Higher-Performing Teams

When a team takes ownership of its problems,
the problem gets solved. It is true on the battlefield,
it is true in business, and it is true in life.
—JOCKO WILLINK

When reading about the founding of our nation and the actions of young Colonel George Washington during the French and Indian War, I found that in 1755 Washington led a group Virginians, along with British troops, into battle, and they suffered enormous losses.

Remarkably, George Washington was the only mounted officer not shot down off his horse, and he had been quite vulnerable to injury since he bravely rode back and forth along the front lines, engaging his troops.

After arriving back at Fort Cumberland, he described what had occurred in battle, that when he had removed his jacket at the end of the battle, he discovered it bore four bullet holes but not a single bullet had touched him. The story of the divine protection of Washington spread across the colonies.

When you *engage* your employees and focus on doing the right thing (like Colonel George Washington engaged his troops at the front line) in the day-to-day "battle" of running your business, eventually, you will build a culture where people thrive and profits soar, and you will win the war.

Leaders who involve their people through a leadership approach like Engage2Lead and the questions of 1-2-3 will experience these key benefits.

Better Teamwork

I love to study trends in business. And two trends are clear: operating a business has grown increasingly complex, and the organizational structure of companies has become flatter, requiring greater transparency.

I have also observed that, today, the success of organizations depends more than ever on teamwork (successfully practicing communication, coordination, and cooperation), maintaining and enhancing relationships, and, at the same time, driving for results.

> *No matter how brilliant your mind or strategy, if you're playing a solo game, you'll always lose out to a team.*
> —REID HOFFMAN

One of the best ways to approach flat organizations in a very complex business world and achieve the high calling of your True North is to follow the Engage2Lead approach and use the 1-2-3 practice.

> *Engage2Lead involves asking for and considering employees' input when making decisions, which leads to more informed and better decision-making results.*

The 1-2-3 approach reminds leaders to involve their people, as appropriate, when making important decisions and setting goals. By doing so, every leader can develop a more effective and efficient team that brings consistently better results while maintaining and enhancing relationships.

Your people will embrace your transparency, and they will get really excited to help you manage your flat organization in a complex business world for results.

Better Learning through Experience

Have you ever heard the statement, "The teacher learns more than his students"? For over thirty years, I have been teaching high school boys at my church. And I've been surprised by how much I have learned, just in my preparation time, and how much I've retained—long after the lesson is taught. And the same holds true for business: more engagement means more learning.

The training and development of our people was an important part of our business, and we monitored its effectiveness. In fact, our chief operating officer would often say, "Training has not occurred until behaviors have changed."

Tell me and I forget. Teach me and I remember.
Involve me and I learn.
—SOURCE UNKNOWN

Our knowledge and our abilities are largely determined not by our IQ or some other fixed measure of intelligence but by the effectiveness of our learning process—in the experiences of participative learning.

As you engage your team by asking them to participate in the decision-making process, they learn more about the key issues. And they take more ownership and become excited about the challenges and opportunities being considered.

Their knowledge and ownership of the project, and the resulting energy, propel them to implement a decision with excellence. And an informed team also experiences fewer surprises as they roll out new initiatives.

Take a True North Bearing

How have you best learned? Would you agree that more engagement means more learning? Are you ready to use the 1-2-3 practice?

A Great Workplace Culture

Building a great workplace culture is not about what you get but what you give. It is not what you get *from* your employees. It is what you give *to* your people. Prior to selling my company, which employed over one hundred fifty people, to a publicly traded company, it was rare that any of us ever used the word *culture*. And it was even rarer that we said the words *employee engagement*.

Why? Because we understood that . . .

Culture is the fruit and not the goal.

When culture becomes your goal, you know that you have crossed the line to what you are going to get *from* your employees. You might even engage your employees to enhance relationships, but if you are motivated by what you are going to get from them, you're also missing the mark.

However, as we discussed in chapter 1, we found that when we focused first on doing the right thing in a principled way—meeting the needs of our employees without strings attached—we produced delicious fruit. This fruit took the form of not only a great culture but also extraordinary results (delighted customers and increased profits) as you'll see in the final benefit in this chapter.

Touch a heart before you ask for a hand.
—JOHN MAXWELL

Like most organizations, we had a standard organizational chart with me at the top of the chart. As you know, this type of organizational chart signals to the employees that they are here to serve the person at the top of the organization—that was me.

However, we took on an attitude of an *upside-down* organizational chart where I was at the bottom of the chart. And it was my responsibility to serve and equip the leaders who reported to me, and it was their responsibility to serve and equip those who reported to them . . . and so on, until we reached the frontline people.

The neat thing about this different approach was the *customer* was the one actually at the top of the organizational chart. All our people knew well that all of our time, energy, and effort were to serve the customer.

To accomplish this internal focus on our employees, we consistently looked at how we could serve our people in a holistic way: mind, body, spirit, and emotions (or relationships). In other words, our focus was on what we could give to our people, not what we were going to get from them. In doing so, we found we had . . .

A culture where people thrived and profits soared.

For those leaders who believe this sounds too soft, let me assure you again that our people clearly understood my drive for results. They understood Bobby Albert expected them to perform at their highest level of excellence, and at the same time, they understood Bobby truly cared for them as people.

Fruit trees usually take two to five years to produce their first fruit. As a leader, though, you can begin the process today when you engage your employees. By consistently using the Engage2Lead participative leadership style and the 1-2-3 practice, in time, the process will produce delicious fruit.

Better-Informed Decisions

When using a participative leadership style like Engage2Lead and a process like 1-2-3, you'll also make better-informed decisions. When facing a decision, your personal insight will seldom be as broad and deep as that of your team. Your people are in a position to know what kinds of things might get in the way of implementing decisions that are made and plans that are laid out. Their input will smooth the way for implementation or execution of the decisions and plans.

As the leader, you have now afforded yourself more resources, ideas, and energy than you would have had on your own. You can devise better and more diverse alternatives when your team provides you multiple perspectives on how to reach your decision.

Employee Ownership of Decisions

When you sincerely solicit your employees' thoughts and ideas, they are more likely to see themselves as full-fledged members of an outstanding team. Instead of feeling like "just a clerk, helper, janitor, receptionist, etc.," they feel valued and important to the overall success of the organization. As a team, they will share in the credit for victories and the blame for losses, and they will be prepared to weather the impact of decisions and plans.

And, if you implement participative decision making, your employees are going to get excited about being asked for their ideas and involvement. They will also have a better understanding of and commitment to the decisions that they collaboratively set. They will be your biggest cheerleaders, and they will bring results far beyond your expectations.

What an excellent way for your people to feel a sense of achievement and to earn recognition for that achievement—all because they were involved in the development and implementation of decisions made. And your organization will reach a level of team-initiated accomplishment that was impossible before using this process.

You also automatically eliminate a good deal of resistance to new ideas. Instead of resisting edicts that come down from on high, employees will support and even champion the decisions that arise from the more participative Engage2Lead approach.

Take a True North Bearing

Do your employees think like owners? Have you struggled to get your people to support your decisions? What might happen in your organization if you started to make decisions with the help of your team?

Eliminate Obstacles

Will employees on the front line, supervisors, and middle managers have to carry out decisions made by those who do the planning? Of course they will! And who are better positioned than they to know what kinds of things might get in the way of implementing decisions and plans?

Better Results

Earlier, I said that all leaders want three things:

1. Results
2. Results
3. Results!

I think it is human nature for leaders to strive to lead their people toward greater results. And I also think it is common for leaders to encounter some pushback from their people. Here's the good news: there is an effective way to minimize this resistance and establish a high level of engagement in any team. And the solution is available to every leader.

Here's some more insight into human nature: people want to be heard and understood by their leader. A popular quote, often attributed to Theodore Roosevelt, illustrates my point:

People don't care how much you know until they know how much you care.

Now, this concept may seem elementary, but elementary truths often offer great gain while hiding in plain sight.

As we said in chapter 2, fully effective leaders understand that, as you drive for results, it is equally important to build, maintain, and enhance positive relationships by engaging your people. It's a matter of all teammates banding together with mutual respect, trust, understanding, and commitment to the organization's goals.

When you, as a leader, engage your employees, you will experience results similar to those detailed in Gallup's 2016 State of the American Workplace report, which I referenced earlier. After analyzing surveys from over one million employees, they found that teams scoring in the top quartile of engagement outperform teams scoring in the bottom quartile by realizing:

- 20 percent higher sales
- 24 percent lower turnover in high-turnover organizations
- 59 percent lower turnover in low-turnover organizations
- 41 percent less absenteeism
- 70 percent fewer employee safety incidents[21]

Rather than constantly focusing on results, focus on the people who will give you the results.

I can tell you that once I began to include our people in the decision-making process, I was able to build a peak-performance team that achieved extraordinary

---

21   Gallup, "State of the American Workplace 2016," p. 68.

results. I was able to maximize my team's potential and minimize their weakness when achieving results. And we did more as a team than we would have if I had made decisions alone. In contrast, if you lead like a Lone Ranger, your strengths and weaknesses are more exposed.

It makes sense: all of the above benefits naturally produce peak performance when decision making involves leaders and employees at all levels within the organization. And an informed team also experiences fewer surprises as they roll out new initiatives.

Take a True North Bearing

Do you spend a lot of time just selling a decision to your people? Have you considered including your people, at the beginning of the decision-making process, before you make a decision?

Achieving better results also has to do with activating all five key concepts of the Path of Effective Leadership: leading and managing; relationships and results; process and content; principles rather than expediency; and goals and controls.

For example, let's say a leader announces a new goal or product/service offering. All leaders must first focus on results, which drive the content (what they want to say and do).

After the new goal or offering is announced, leaders have a choice. They must decide how much they want to invest in the process (how they say and do it—including how they involve/engage people in decision making). Results-oriented managers are focused on reaching the end goal and how to reach it most efficiently. They focus very little on process (how they interact and involve/engage people). These managers devote much energy and time during the implementation phase. This extra effort is required in order to convince the team to get on board with an implementation plan—which they had very little to do with forming.

In contrast, the relationship-oriented leader is focused on achieving the desired goal as effectively as possible. These leaders realize that the relationships built and fostered among the team make a huge impact on the ultimate outcomes. They focus on how they say and do things as they press toward the goal. They spend more time, up front, with their team, soliciting opinions, brainstorming, and asking questions, following the process of goals and controls.

They do spend more time focused on the process of engaging employees, but they enjoy a smoother and shorter implementation phase due to the high level of ownership and engagement that results from this type of approach.

Results-oriented manager approach

Relationship-oriented leader approach

The up-front time invested in relationship-oriented leadership yields notably better results.

The results-oriented approach might show results sooner than the relationship-oriented approach; however, any early advances of a results-focused approach will be eclipsed by a high-performing, unified team led by a relationship-oriented leader. And, in some cases, the results-focused approach will produce negative results because of poor implementation.

Through trial and error and employing the process of "crawl-walk-run," I've learned that focusing on good process (engaging employees through relationships) is the best way to obtain the desired result, and I have grown to absolutely trust the process of the relationship-oriented approach to leadership. In fact, if you want to hit a full stride with your leadership effectiveness, I highly recommend this approach.

Why? Because when I trust good process, I always get good results—plus all the other benefits of people being involved in the process, such as . . .

- Buy-in
- Ownership
- Becoming cheerleaders of the decision

And, of course, when things get stressful, effective leaders take the time to remember their principles, rather than simply do what is expedient.

Take a True North Bearing

Are you a results-oriented manager or a relationship-oriented leader who is also focused on achieving results? What steps can you take today to start earning the enthusiasm, initiative, and devotion of your employees?

As the leader, you don't have to know it all any longer. You can experience all of the benefits of an engaged team with Engage2Lead and 1-2-3.

CHAPTER 19

The Consequences of Poor Leadership

*Destructive Aftershocks Always Follow the
Fault Line of Ineffective Leadership*

> *As a leader every action has a consequence.*
> *Make sure it is the one you intend.*
> —KATHERINE BRYANT

If you're like most leaders I've talked with, you probably believe you have some very good reasons for not involving your employees in your decision-making process. Let's consider a few excuses I've heard.

Common Excuses for Not Involving Employees in Decision Making

1. "It never occurred to me that I should."

This is one of the more common reasons I've heard—and the most inexcusable.

2. "I'm the leader, so I'm in charge."

Bright, knowledgeable, dedicated, decisive, and dependable leaders can also be impatient and intolerant when dealing with others. Consequently, they assume that no one else in the organization could possibly contribute toward a better decision or plan. Ouch! Sound familiar? As you learned in the last chapter, the paradox is that such leaders often find themselves isolated and, therefore, ignorant of how to best solve problems in the first place.

3. "I don't have time."

More like, "I didn't *take* time," which is usually unjustifiable. Most leaders sincerely believe it takes too much time and effort to adopt a more participative (engaging), relationship-oriented leadership style.

> *If you don't have time to do it right, when will you have time to do it over?*
> —JOHN WOODEN

And most leaders think they have to give up the drive for results to invest in the Engage2Lead process. Consequently, they miss out on enhanced relationships with their people and greater financial results for their organization.

This approach is too difficult to understand, they think, and they say to themselves, "I've got work to do, and my people need to be working. Besides, I pay my people top dollar, and they don't need to be sitting around talking."

Take a True North Bearing

As a leader, do you think you have time in your schedule to ask for input and decision-making help from your employees?

Here's another paradox: what may seem to be "extra and unnecessary" time and effort devoted to a participative leadership approach actually opens the door to achieving the results we have pursued for so long.

However, at least in the workplace, it takes incredibly little additional time and effort to allow others

- To contribute their thoughts on pending decisions
- To encourage involvement
- To ask for commitments instead of demanding them
- To be constructive and supportive when seeking improvement
- To be able to disagree without being disagreeable
- To capitalize on the creative ideas and support of all those who can contribute to making good things happen

Only a few people learn to focus on the skills to both build relationships (how they say and do/engaging employees) and get results (what they say and do)—not simply one or the other. This is the leader employees long to work for, and when they find one, they usually give their loyalty to the leader and make that job a career.

Adopting the principles of the process of employee engagement (relationships) and results will take some extra time and effort, but the results will far exceed the additional investment in yourself and others.

> *It takes less time to do a thing right, than it does to explain why you did it wrong.*
> —HENRY WADSWORTH LONGFELLOW

4. "It's not my job!"

Wow! Who has neglected to properly select, induct, train, and coach this manager about the importance of teamwork? Good teamwork should automatically be understood to be an important part of everyone's job.

And, unfortunately, there are the occasional situations when self-serving people, to get their own way, intentionally proceed on their own. They would rather apologize later than initially seek permission and acceptance.

5. "I'm already getting enough input from my people."

Some leaders think that they do *include* their people as they make decisions but, in reality, don't truly *involve* their people in a meaningful way. These leaders ask (on a limited basis) their employees to offer input for ideas to the problems, challenges, and opportunities they are experiencing on the front line. They might engage their people in conversation when they cross paths in the office and other work areas. They might even call folks, one at a time, into their office to solicit opinions and advice.

These leaders are, in fact, learning about some of the underlying problems in their organization as they go about talking to various individuals in the workplace. But, they are missing the significant improvements that result from group discussion and brainstorming around the challenges and opportunities that exist and lie ahead.

6. "I tried it once, and it didn't work."

I wonder how many times this manager fell off his bike before he could ride it well?

The Engage2Lead decision-making process takes practice, practice, practice before it becomes part of the culture and people understand how it works.

Take a True North Bearing

What is your excuse for not employing a more participative leadership style? How does your organization encourage teamwork and collaboration in its decision-making process?

Consequences of Not Using Engage2Lead

As you can see, it's often easy to justify excluding others in our decision-making process. But, the results of a more independent, less inclusive leadership can be devastating to an organization and its people, resulting in some or all of the following negative consequences.

1. Incomplete information

First, you'll make decisions based on incomplete information. As I mentioned before, the bolder and more decisive executives become, the more likely they are to disregard good process and expediently focus on the drive for results. In doing so, they ignore the rich resource of information that can only be found in their frontline people.

Their singular focus on things, and subsequent disregard for people, becomes a trap that hinders their team's effectiveness and ultimately limits their overall results.

2. Save an ounce, but pay a pound

You may save an ounce of effort in one area or department without realizing it will require a pound of effort in one or more other areas or departments.

When we have problems communicating or interacting, we tend to blame the environment or someone else rather than ourselves. Leaders often think that a quick, decisive approach saves time and money, but often they spend far more time on the back-end of the decision, trying to gain buy-in and boost the engagement of their people, like I used to.

How easy it is to settle for an attitude of blame: "I wish the other departments in our company would be more communicative and cooperative with us; I wish others would listen to me."

A leader's results-focused approach becomes a trap that stifles relationships, limits results, and sabotages our best-intended efforts.

3. Lack of inspiration and enthusiasm

Team members will lack inspiration and enthusiasm when being asked to implement something they weren't "in on."

We are generally not "up on" what we are not "in on."

Folks can quickly become disenchanted with supervisors who make decisions unilaterally or expect to be obeyed, simply because they are the boss. Instead of attacking the main issue or opportunity head-on, leaders feel like they're spinning their wheels, trying to gain buy-in from their people.

This understanding affirms the well-known adage, "People don't leave companies; they leave supervisors."

People won't get truly inspired to achieve peak performance unless they are asked for their input on what should be the goals and processes. They want to be respected and invited to use their minds to help the organization.

4. Unhappy employees

Unsuitable approaches result in unhappy employees at all levels of the organization. This is especially true on the front lines, when folks are repeatedly asked to carry out decisions in ways that they know are not as effective or efficient as they could be.

The more capable and dedicated employees are, the more frustrated they will be with unilateral, nonparticipative leadership.

Likewise, the supervisors and managers are unhappy that the people reporting to them aren't more excited and enthusiastic about carrying out their responsibilities. Can you just see the dog trying to chase his tail?

5. People feel used

It's only natural for employees at all levels in an organization to feel like they are being perceived as only tools rather than as knowledgeable, thinking individuals. The result is that they rapidly become uninspired, unmotivated employees.

When we relegate people to carrying out someone else's orders, we prevent them from having a full measure of opportunity to achieve. They typically choose fight, flight, or submission in response. Management must understand that to refuse to involve employees, even in the simplest of activities, will only serve to discredit a people-first culture.

Take a True North Bearing

Has a primarily results-focused approach trapped you into strained relationships and disappointing outcomes? Based on your calendar and daily agenda, which do you value more: people or things?

Have I convinced you yet of the value of Engage2Lead and 1-2-3? If so, I have just one more participative leadership concept to share with you: the One-Over-One policy.

CHAPTER 20

The One-Over-One Policy

*A Simple Way to Boost
Your Team's Morale and Trust*

*Trust is the highest form of human motivation.
It brings out the very best in people.*
—STEPHEN R. COVEY

As the years went by, my company began to optimize results with our Engage2Lead decision-making approach and the 1-2-3 leadership practice.

I was very excited at how empowered our frontline employees felt to make decisions and how inspired and enthusiastic they were. They behaved as though they were the owners of the organization.

Then, one day, I heard a few employees grumbling and questioning a frontline supervisor. The supervisor had moved a high-performing employee to a larger, empty, seemingly extra workstation. We were actually saving that workstation for another future frontline supervisor yet to be hired, and that supervisor hadn't asked *her* supervisor about using the workstation.

As the leader of your organization, division, function, or department, what would you do to resolve the situation?

- You could ask the supervisor to move the employee back to their previous workstation. This decision would reduce the grumbling and questioning, but you would risk losing an excellent employee over breaking the supervisor's promise and trust.

- You could allow the employee to remain at the larger workstation so the supervisor does not damage the relationship with her employee over a broken promise. But, you risk the grumbling and questioning from the other employees getting out of control and spreading like wildfire. Consequently, you may lose other good employees.

Is this situation beginning to feel like leadership checkmate?

Take a True North Bearing

Have you ever encountered a situation at work where someone was told they should expect a raise, a promotion, or other perk and it didn't come, leaving the employee with hurt feelings? What did you do?

Another day while I was talking with a leadership team member in my company, I just happened to ask about a project assigned to one of our very creative and empowered frontline employees. Upon further investigation, we discovered that the employee was in the process of procuring tens of thousands of dollars of materials and equipment, without even asking for feedback from another coworker or approval from his supervisor. On top of that, we learned that the employee had also

- Changed the look of a registered trademark logo

- Used a color scheme that was completely inconsistent with our corporate marketing image
- Selected equipment, material, and design structure that the supplier highly recommended we *not* use
- Used a wrong phone number in the marketing messaging for potential customers to call

Yikes! Immediately, our leadership team member asked the employee to "place the order on hold" so other people on our leadership team could look over his decision.

As the CEO of a growing company, I quickly discovered that the leadership role comes with its share of challenges. Sometimes leaders feel as if they are herding cats. One of the principal tasks of leaders is to unify the efforts of their team to achieve common goals. It takes a clear vision, open communication (both vertically and horizontally), and a lot of patient reinforcement to get everyone playing from the same sheet of music.

When you order a box of pens to later discover that you ordered the wrong pens, you can return them. However, when we make a wrong decision when supervising employees, it is hard to put the genie back in the bottle and return to where things were.

My mother used to say, "An ounce of prevention is worth a pound of cure." We have all heard that saying, and I think you would agree with me that Mom was right. That is why we ask our children to move their milk glass away from the edge of the dinner table. We know that a misplaced elbow can quickly push the glass off the table, and we understand the time and effort involved with cleaning up the spill. It's so much easier to prevent a problem than deal with the mess that follows a mishap.

Over the years, I discovered that there were ways to avoid "spilled milk" in our business. One of my company's best Human Resource (HR) policies provided a simple way to prevent this type of misunderstanding between supervisors and employees.

Take a True North Bearing

How do you address the kind of situation mentioned above
in your organization? Has your approach been effective?

A Simple Human Resource Policy to the Rescue

Eventually, I instituted an HR policy called One-Over-One to help address this very problem.

> *The One-Over-One policy states that any decision regarding branding, procedures, procurement, or personnel matters must first be discussed with, and agreed upon by, the supervisor one level above the supervisor making the decision.*

So, *before* a supervisor tells an employee that he is going to receive a raise, promotion, or working-condition perk (e.g., larger work area, a special chair, a printer in his workstation, a special office, etc.), the supervisor must first speak with her supervisor one level above and get approval.

This simple policy helps manage the expectations of everyone involved, especially the hard-working employee who deserves the respect of accurate communication regarding these matters. And I have found that managing everyone's expectations does boost job satisfaction.

These potential problems exist in every organization. The good news is that all leaders can improve the morale and effectiveness of their organization by adopting this straightforward policy.

Why Does One-Over-One Work?

This policy seems like common sense, and it is. So, you might wonder why you should have a policy like One-Over-One.

1. We've all heard the saying, "Two heads are better than one." This policy encourages our people to reap the rewards of this valuable principle, allowing us to lead our organizations to higher effectiveness and our employees to greater job satisfaction.
2. Leaders can avoid significant, complicated personnel risk, such as when an inappropriate decision must be allowed to stand or the supervisor's decision needs to be reversed. Either of these alternatives can potentially create significant problems.
3. The policy builds confidence and trust between supervisors and their supervisors and between supervisors and employees when the process is explained to employees *only* after the approved decision to give them a raise, or promotion, or working-condition perk.
4. Supervisors and employees become more aware of the importance of the corporate procedures in place.
5. The policy recruits the help of middle- and upper-tier supervisors to help maintain consistency in important areas.
6. The policy allows for creative thought and change while providing guidelines that prevent ineffective or unproductive ideas to grow.
7. The policy leverages the leader's time by providing a structured yet collaborative way to stay the course while providing a roadmap for new ideas and suggestions.
8. The policy encourages mutual accountability.

Imagine being able to better manage the expectations of your supervisors and employees with a simple policy.

Let's return to the situation where the supervisor moved an employee to a larger workstation. Would you like to know what happened after we implemented this policy?

First, our HR team spent time reviewing the new policy with each supervisor who led a team of people. Those supervisors clearly understood to speak with their supervisor before one word or promise was mentioned to an employee about receiving a raise, promotion, or working-condition perk. When the supervisor had that conversation to share what benefit the employee was receiving, she also shared the whole process she had gone through so the benefit could be approved. That signaled to the employee the following:

1. The supervisor went to great lengths to ensure the employee would receive the benefit. It developed a trust relationship between them.
2. Even his supervisor's boss also knew how well he was performing in his job and cared for him as well.
3. HR also knew about his performance because it was recorded in their personnel file.
4. In many cases, it was a surprise to the employee because they were already grateful to work in a culture where people thrive and profits soar.
5. The employee knew he was a truly a valuable member of the team.
6. Because of this process, the employee looked forward to coming to work each day, and his performance took another leap forward.
7. It had an unexpected but pleasant wow factor.

The One-Over-One policy will help you prevent spilled milk and reduce misguided efforts in your organization, thus creating more time for you to proactively build and grow your business and guide your team to move forward, not backward.

Take a True North Bearing

Have these types of problems surfaced in your organization? Will you consider using the One-Over-One HR policy as a way to effectively prevent spilled milk with your team?

I am often asked if decision making is top-down or bottom-up. The answer is both. The *participative approach* of Engage2Lead and 1-2-3 is usually considered a top-down effective decision-making process. The leader is the one who initiates the process and taps the best ideas from both the leader and the frontline people.

However, the One-Over-One policy is an example of a bottom-up effective decision-making process, where a supervisor initiates the process and obtains the approval from her supervisor one level above.

1-2-3 = More Engagement and Better Decisions

I have found a completely different atmosphere exists in a workplace with an Engage2Lead-sensitive leader who respects his subordinates and who has the good sense to seek and appreciate input from employees.

With the 1-2-3 leadership practice guiding a participatory decision-making approach, employees can enjoy being respected for sharing their ideas. They can not only become truly inspired but also enhance the organization's chances for success by virtue of their input.

I have also found engaged employees are enthusiastic about their work, show initiative, and loyally devote themselves to further the organization's reputation and interest. This extra level of effort and contribution is called discretionary effort.

When you, as the leader, earn such discretionary effort from your team, you have found the goose that lays the golden eggs.

To sum up, with Engage2Lead and 1-2-3, you can see the following benefits:

1. *Employees feel good about themselves* because they have a sense of achievement and enjoy receiving recognition for their accomplishments.

2. *Employees really appreciate being appreciated.* They feel useful, and they welcome the opportunity to participate in any decision related to their operations. They enjoy being respected as useful professionals whose opinions are important. They are excited to be respected as valuable thinkers as well as doers.

3. *Customers appreciate being dealt with respectfully* and are delighted because delighted employees enthusiastically serve them.

4. *Employees become truly inspired* and enhance the organization's chances for success by virtue of their input.

5. *Morale and teamwork increase*, which leads to improved performance and optimum results. The leader's impact is multiplied, not merely added.

6. *There is buy-in and ownership* because employees are involved in the decision-making process. Through their early participation, people gain informal pretraining (knowledge and perspective) that helps them effectively implement the decision. It's no wonder such folks become cheerleaders of the decision.

7. *Employees gain a better understanding of the results they are expected to achieve* when invited to engage in the process. They also are likely to understand why it is important to achieve these results.

8. *Employees who are part of the process feel their opinion is valued* and are more likely to be committed to working within the team to achieve the results.

9. *Employees' performance is enhanced.* They come to work on time daily, have a good attendance record, work for a higher purpose, and give a full day's work for their pay.

10. *Organizations experience both highly motivated employees and high-performance teams* as all of these factors come together.

You can buy someone's time, you can buy someone's physical presence at a given place, you can even buy a measured number of skilled muscular motions per hour or day. But, you cannot buy enthusiasm; you cannot buy initiative; you cannot buy loyalty; you cannot buy devotion of hearts, minds, and souls. You have to earn these things.
—CLARENCE FRANCIS

CONCLUSION

Continuing the Journey

As I wrap up this book, my thoughts turn to true north—that unchanging reference point for all geographic navigation around the world.

We have learned that organizations need reference points, navigation tools, and provisions for the journey through the marketplace.

I have unveiled five important aspects of leading that I call the True North Business Essentials.

- Our *core values* and our *purpose* comprise our compass, based on our organization's unchanging truths.
- Our *vision* communicates to our people and the world where we are headed.
- Our *super-objectives* give our team a clear picture of what must be accomplished every day to make it to our envisioned future.
- The *effective leadership* principles and strategies detailed in part one of the book allow us to effectively lead our teams within the guidelines of our core values and purpose on a journey toward our vision of the future.

And we learned about three practices that help us tangibly lead our people well.

1. ON/IN reminds us that while we are often pulled to work *in* our business, we must make time for the important (but often non-urgent) tasks of working *on* our business.
2. WOW! enables us to clearly determine why we exist (our purpose) and where we are going (our vision).
3. 1-2-3 equips us with a tangible way to model participative leadership through a simple decision-making protocol that yields more employee engagement and better decisions.

In summary, this book contains the roadmap, navigation tools, and practical leadership practices to progress forward as a leader, a team, and an organization. I urge you to define your True North, clarify your vision, define your super-objectives, and effectively lead your people using the principles and practices contained in this book. In fact, you may want to lead others in your organization through a study of the truths found here.

Much like a treasure locked in a safety-deposit box does not bring tangible value to its owner, this information will not add value to you unless you employ it in your life and business. Please don't slide this book onto your bookshelf and lock away its promise of value. I urge you to underline, highlight, and dog-ear these pages as you reference them to guide you toward the extraordinary growth and impact you've sought for so long.

ACKNOWLEDGMENTS

I would like to thank all of the people who, over many years, made me look better than I really am:

To Jim Lundy, who was my long-term executive mentor and friend and who took a young, ambitious leader and chipped away the imperfections to make me better.

To our people of the Albert Companies, each and every one, who gave their all to make our company the best.

To Brady Beshear, our chief operating officer for my new company, Values-Driven Leadership, who speaks truth to me when I need it and has taken my raw writings and made this manuscript look really good.

To Amanda Rooker, the developmental writer who shaped this manuscript into a better representation of my intended message.

To the folks at Morgan James Publishing: David Hancock, Aubrey Kincaid, and my good friend Karen Anderson, and the rest of the team who labored to bring this book into the world.

ABOUT THE AUTHOR

Bobby Albert is a workplace culture and leadership expert and author of *True North Business* and *Principled Profits*. Founder of Values-Driven Leadership and former CEO of the Albert Companies, Bobby is a lifelong entrepreneur, having started or acquired over twenty businesses. The 100 Best Companies to Work for in Texas awarded their coveted designation to the Albert team for the first two years they applied for consideration.

As a regular contributor on Fox News Radio, he provides insight on leadership, workplace culture, and employee engagement. Bobby is a leadership mentor and workplace culture consultant, helping other organizations embrace the powerful truths presented in *True North Business*. A cycling enthusiast, Bobby has logged almost 100,000 miles on his road bike. He and his wife, Susan, live in north Texas and have three married sons and eight grandchildren.

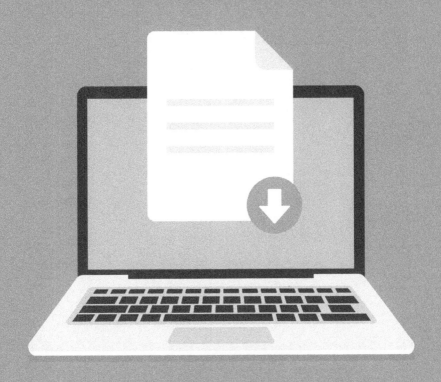

Want to Launch Your Leadership to the Next Level?

Get on board with Lead to Grow Mentoring with Bobby Albert!

GO TO

BobbyAlbert.com/LtoGmentoring

SPEAKING

Help Your People Achieve Meaningful
SUCCESS

Looking for your next keynote speaker?

INQUIRE AT

BobbyAlbert.com/Speaking

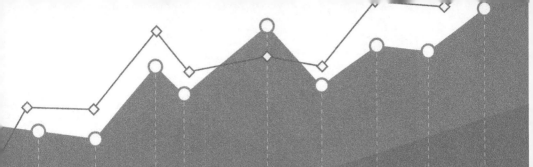

LEAD TO GROW

with Bobby Albert

PODCAST

Leaders are Learners!

Learn from the best as Bobby interviews leaders from across the nation.

SUBSCRIBE IN ITUNES AND LEARN MORE AT

BobbyAlbert.com/LtoGpodcast